ALCOHOL ABUSE

Other books in the At Issue series:

Affirmative Action
Animal Experimentation
Anti-Semitism
The Attack on America:
    September 11, 2001
Bulimia
The Central Intelligence
    Agency
Child Labor and Sweatshops
Child Sexual Abuse
Cloning
Creationism vs. Evolution
Date Rape
Does Capital Punishment
    Deter Crime?
Drunk Driving
The Ethics of Euthanasia
Ethnic Conflict
Food Safety
The Future of the Internet
Gay Marriage
Guns and Crime
Home Schooling
How Can Gun Violence Be
    Reduced?
Human Embryo Research
Immigration Policy
Interracial Relationships
Is Global Warming a Threat?
Is Media Violence a Problem?
Islamic Fundamentalism
Legalizing Drugs
Marijuana

The Media and Politics
Missile Defense
National Security
Organ Transplants
Performance Enhancing Drugs
Physician-Assisted Suicide
Police Corruption
Professional Wrestling
Rain Forests
Rape on Campus
Satanism
School Shootings
Sex Education
Sexually Transmitted Diseases
Should Abortion Rights Be
    Restricted?
Should There Be Limits on
    Free Speech?
Single-Parent Families
Smoking
The Spread of AIDS
Teen Sex
Teen Suicide
UFOs
The United Nations
U.S. Policy Toward China
Video Games
Violent Children
Voting Behavior
Welfare Reform
What Is a Hate Crime?
White Supremacy Groups

ALCOHOL ABUSE

HaiSong Harvey, *Book Editor*

Daniel Leone, *President*
Bonnie Szumski, *Publisher*
Scott Barbour, *Managing Editor*

AT ISSUE

OPPOSING VIEWPOINTS® SERIES

GREENHAVEN PRESS®

THOMSON
™
GALE

San Diego • Detroit • New York • San Francisco • Cleveland
New Haven, Conn. • Waterville, Maine • London • Munich

© 2003 by Greenhaven Press. Greenhaven Press is an imprint of The Gale Group, Inc., a division of Thomson Learning, Inc.

Greenhaven® and Thomson Learning™ are trademarks used herein under license.

For more information, contact
Greenhaven Press
27500 Drake Rd.
Farmington Hills, MI 48331-3535
Or you can visit our Internet site at http://www.gale.com

LIBRARY OF CONGRESS CATALOGING-IN-PUBLICATION DATA

Alcohol abuse / HaiSong Harvey, book editor.
    p. cm. — (At issue)
Includes bibliographical references and index.
ISBN 0-7377-1159-0 (pbk. : alk. paper) — ISBN 0-7377-1160-4 (hb : alk. paper)
    1. Alcoholism. 2. Alcoholics—Rehabilitation. I. Harvey, HaiSong. II. At issue (San Diego, Calif.)
HV5035 .A447 2003
362.292—dc21   2002023620

Printed in the United States of America

Contents

Page

Introduction   6

1. Alcoholism Is a Disease   9
   Katherine Ketcham et al.

2. Alcoholism Is Not a Disease   14
   Edward A. Dreyfus

3. Alcoholics Anonymous Is the Best Treatment for   20
   Alcoholics
   Thomas Curtis Chace

4. Alcoholics Anonymous Is Not the Best Treatment   26
   for Alcoholics
   Jack Trimpey

5. Alcoholics Cannot Learn to Drink in Moderation   30
   Mike Harden

6. Alcoholics Can Learn to Drink in Moderation   33
   Stanton Peele

7. Colleges Should Promote Tougher Policies Against   40
   Alcohol Abuse
   Henry Wechsler, Toben Nelson, and Elissa R. Weitzman

8. Colleges Should Promote Moderate Drinking   48
   Franklin B. Krohn

9. Drug Therapy Is an Effective Treatment for Alcohol Abuse   55
   Donald W. Goodwin

Organizations to Contact   63

Bibliography   69

Index   72

Introduction

In ancient Greece the festival of Anthesteria was a four-day long celebration of feast and worship in honor of Dionysus, the god of wine. This time of merriment included the consumption of wine as well as the welcomed effects of intoxication. The festival would end on a more sobering note as the ancient Greeks made atonement and rejoiced in the resurrection and return of Dionysus.

In modern times, people have continued this tradition of consuming alcohol in celebration on holidays or at other joyous occasions, such as weddings. However, for many people alcohol is a source of misery and pain. For these individuals, alcohol is not a symbol of merriment, but rather a vice and an obsession that consumes them.

In the United States alone, approximately 14 million people combat some form of alcohol abuse. Alcohol abuse is broadly defined as a destructive pattern of alcohol use. Under this definition, excessive or "binge" drinking is a form of alcohol abuse, since it can cause the drinker to experience physical illness, blackouts, and even death. In addition, individuals may engage in violent or irresponsible behavior while intoxicated. Drunk driving is also a form of alcohol abuse, since it may harm both the drinker and others. The abuse of alcohol can have severe implications on one's personal, occupational, and social life. Alcohol abuse is prevalent among men, women, and teenagers alike.

Alcohol abuse and alcoholism

Some alcohol abusers, but not all, are alcoholics: Of the approximately 14 million alcohol abusers in America, it is estimated that slightly less than 7 million are alcoholics. Alcoholism is the most severe form of alcohol abuse. Whereas alcohol abuse is defined as the destructive use of alcohol, alcoholism is the destructive addiction to alcohol. Alcoholism is characterized by the repeated, obsessive, and uncontrollable use of alcohol despite extremely negative consequences.

Alcoholism has long been accepted as a debilitating disease to which some people are more disposed to than others. Elvin M. Jellinek, of the Yale Center of Alcohol Studies, first popularized the disease concept of alcoholism in 1960. He maintained that alcoholism is a progressive, life-threatening disease. He also stated that individuals who suffered from this disease could never drink in moderation, and that complete abstinence from alcohol was the only healthy choice for alcoholics.

Since then, physicians, researchers and policymakers have accepted that alcoholism is indeed a disease. According to the National Institute on Alcohol Abuse and Alcoholism (NIAAA), "Alcoholism is a chronic, often progressive disease with symptoms that include a strong need to drink despite negative consequences, such as serious job or health problems. Like many other diseases, it has a generally predictable course, has recognized symptoms, and is influenced by both genetic and environmental factors that are being increasingly well defined." Today, the majority of treatment options for alcoholism, and some forms of alcohol abuse, are based on this disease theory.

However, there is opposition to this widely accepted view that alcoholism is a disease. Herbert Fingarette argues in his book *Heavy Drinking: The Myth of Alcoholism as a Disease* that the disease theory is ambiguous and contradictory, and therefore has been abandoned by most scientists and researchers. Fingarette believes that by defining alcoholism as a disease, the medical community sends a message that alcoholism is purely physical and that the individual alcoholic is not responsible for his or her compulsive behavior. Fingarette also warns that the disease theory thwarts treatment because it establishes alcoholics as victims of a disease that they cannot control and yet tells them to learn to control it with abstinence.

Alcoholics Anonymous and its critics

One of the biggest supporters of the disease theory is Alcoholics Anonymous (AA). AA is a well-known recovery group for alcoholics and alcohol abusers. AA, which was founded in 1935, has helped thousands of alcoholics over the years and now boasts over 2 million members across the globe. AA describes itself as a "fellowship of men and women who share their experience, strength and hope with each other that they may solve their common problem and help others to recover from alcoholism."

AA is based on a series of 12 steps. These famous 12 steps, which have become the foundations for many other recovery programs, are often viewed as a series of confessions, the first of which is the alcoholic's admission that he or she is powerless over alcohol. Other steps require alcoholics to submit to a "higher power," leading some critics to charge that AA forces its own form of religion on its members. Supporters of AA insist that while the 12 steps lead alcoholics on a spiritual path to recovery, AA itself is not affiliated with any particular religion.

AA's meetings are the foundation of the organization. AA functions with two kinds of meetings: open and closed meetings. Open meetings are open to everyone—alcoholics, their families, friends and anyone wanting to find out information on solving a drinking problem. Closed meetings are only for alcoholics who come together to share and discuss their experiences with alcoholism and the steps for achieving recovery. AA prides itself on being committed to recovery, anonymity, and openness.

Over the years, AA has become an icon of treatment, synonymous with recovery from alcohol abuse. The majority of professionals in medicine and therapy consider AA to be the most successful treatment program for alcoholism and alcohol abuse. In fact, almost all major substance abuse and public health organizations advise most alcohol abusers to seek help with AA.

Members of AA have also been influential in spreading the word about AA. Many of these members have gone on to write books on their experiences with AA. Meredith Gould, author of *Staying Sober: Tips for Working a Twelve Step Program of Recovery*, states in her book, "Of course . . . there are recovery programs around that are purportedly less sexist, more secular, less structured, and more permissive. [However,] at the same time, I know that Twelve Step programs are exactly what doctors, psychotherapists, social workers and clergy invariably recommend after everything else has failed."

However, despite its worldwide acclaim and proposed success in helping alcohol abusers, scientific research studies have failed to support AA's success rate. While there are numerous accounts of individual alcoholics who have achieved sobriety through the 12 steps, research studies designed to measure whether AA members have better recovery rates than nonmembers have been ambiguous at best.

This lack of evidence has led critics to question whether or not AA is truly a panacea for alcohol abuse and alcoholism. Stanton Peele, a lawyer, researcher, and activist well known for his controversial opinions, argues against the disease model of alcoholism, which is fundamental to AA. Peele also takes issue with the AA view that abstinence is the only way to recover from alcoholism. Instead, Peele believes that moderation is an alternative solution for many alcohol abusers.

In *Alcoholics Anonymous: The Unseen Cult*, F. Alexander and M. Rollins write, "AA teaches that the only way for an alcoholic to recover is total abstinence, a demonstrably false assertion accepted on faith." Advocates of moderate drinking believe that AA's abstinence-only proscription is a one-size-fits-all approach to a complex issue. An individual's alcoholism or abuse of alcohol, they argue, may be due to a variety of physical, emotional, and psychological reasons. Abstinence may be the only recourse for some alcoholics, but some heavy or irresponsible drinkers may simply need to learn how to control the amount they drink.

Alcoholics Anonymous, as well as the much talked about disease theory of alcoholism, are just two of the debates surrounding alcohol abuse. The essays in *At Issue: Alcohol Abuse* explore these and other issues relating to the prevention and treatment of alcohol abuse.

1

Alcoholism Is a Disease

Katherine Ketcham and William F. Asbury with Mel Schulstad and Arthur P. Ciaramicoli

Katherine Ketcham is the author of Under the Influence: A Guide to Myths and Realities of Alcoholism. *William F. Asbury is a journalist and former editor-in-chief of the* Seattle Post-Intelligencer. *Mel Schulstad is the cofounder and former president of the National Association of Alcoholism and Drug Abuse Counselors. Arthur P. Ciaramicoli is a licensed clinical psychologist.*

Alcoholism has been viewed as a shameful personal weakness and not as a debilitating disease. However, research studies have shown that alcoholism is in fact a genetically determined disease. In 1990 Kenneth Blum, who spent years searching for the specific genetic markers for the disease of alcoholism, finally found a genetic mutation on chromosome 11 that greatly increases an individual's risk of developing alcoholism. Although this discovery did not hold all the answers for the genetic basis of alcoholism, it provided substantial evidence that indeed alcoholism is a disease.

For hundreds, even thousands of years, people have argued loud and long that alcoholism is a shameful personal weakness, a stubborn character defect, or a symptom of some underlying moral disorder. Alcoholics, because they "choose" their fate (unlike the innocent victims of epilepsy, heart disease, or cancer), rank low in the moral order. "Every human soul is worth saving," proclaimed J.E. Todd more than a hundred years ago in a tract titled *Drunkenness a Vice Not a Disease*, "but . . . if a choice is to be made, drunkards are about the last class to be taken hold of."

Despite stunning advances in our understanding of the genetics and neurophysiology of alcoholism, most people continue to believe that alcoholism is a disease of morals, a preventable psychological "weakness." In a 1979 survey, 67 percent of 2,187 respondents insisted that alcoholism is a sign of "personal emotional weakness"; only 19 percent believed that alcoholism is solely a health problem. A 1998 survey by the San Francisco–based Recovery Institute reveals that our attitudes toward alcoholics have not changed significantly over the years. The survey, which is based on telephone and one-on-one interviews with more than two thousand people, concludes:

> Most people see alcoholism as having elements of both disease and weakness. On average, fewer than one in four say it is 100 percent disease, while a majority of every group surveyed—except psychiatrists and counselors—say they consider alcoholism to be at least 25 percent due to personal or moral weakness.

> Not surprisingly, counselors (70 percent disease, 20 percent weakness) and psychiatrists (77 percent disease, 19 percent weakness) are most likely to accept alcoholism as a medical condition while fundamentalist clergy (31 percent disease, 69 percent weakness) overwhelmingly report seeing alcoholism as a reflection of a shortcoming in character or morality.

> When we dig even deeper and ask in effect whether, because alcoholism is a disease, we therefore can absolve the alcoholic of responsibility for the problem, the answer is a resounding "no" . . . when pressed, most [people] ascribe a very significant degree of volition to the condition of alcoholism.

The shame and stigma associated with alcoholism have persisted despite the fact that we know, from hundreds of studies conducted by thousands of researchers, that alcoholism is a progressive, physiological, genetically determined disease and not a moral or personal weakness. Over the past sixty years, roughly dating from the foundation of the Yale Center of Alcohol Studies in 1942, neurologists, pharmacologists, geneticists, biochemists, psychologists, psychiatrists, and, most recently, addiction medicine specialists (sometimes called "addictionologists"), have amassed a broad assortment of research projects confirming the hereditary, biochemical, and neurophysiological nature of alcoholism.

One of these researchers is pharmacologist Kenneth Blum, who became interested in alcoholism in the late 1960s when he was working as an assistant research scientist at the Southwest Foundation for Research and Education in San Antonio, Texas. Teaming up with psychopharmacologist Irving Geller, Blum began a series of experiments focusing on the nature of alcohol's actions on the nervous system. These early experiments, published in the 1970s, convinced Blum that specific neurotransmitters such as serotonin, GABA, and dopamine are involved in alcohol preference. As the years went by, he became increasingly interested in the actions of alcohol on specific opiate receptor sites in the brain and the neurochemical mechanisms underlying addiction to alcohol.

Quest for the cause

For the next decade Blum teamed up with researchers all over the world to conduct experiments designed to tease apart the mysteries of neurological addiction. By the mid-1980s Blum found himself powerfully drawn to a field of research in which he had no direct training: molecular genetics. Convinced that genes are involved in the craving for alcohol and the predisposition to alcoholism, he wanted to find out which specific genes were causing the problem. With newly discovered techniques such as "pulsed field gel electrophoresis" and "southern blot analysis," researchers were able to identify specific chromosomal markers for certain neurogenetic diseases, including Huntington's disease. Using these same tools, Blum hoped to find specific genetic markers for the neurogenetic disease of alcoholism.

There was no doubt in Blum's mind—or the minds of the men and women he collaborated with in laboratories ranging from California to Colorado, New York, England, and Italy—that alcoholism is a hereditary disease. All you had to do was look at the hundreds of experiments, conducted over more than five decades, confirming the genetic link. Tampering with the genetic code of rodents, researchers were able to breed strains of rats and mice that loved the taste of alcohol and others that couldn't stand the stuff. The DBA and C3H strains of mice, for example, consistently prefer water over alcohol when given a choice, while the C57 and C58 strains will choose alcohol over water almost every time. The offspring of the alcohol-loving rodents inherit this fondness for booze, while the offspring of the alcohol-hating mice simply don't like the stuff.

We know, from hundreds of studies conducted by thousands of researchers, that alcoholism is a progressive, physiological, genetically determined disease.

Adoption studies in humans also provided strong confirmation of the genetic link. In the early 1970s University of Kansas psychiatrist Donald Goodwin and colleagues in America and Denmark published studies conducted with adopted children of alcoholics and nonalcoholics. Children with at least one alcoholic natural parent were three to four times more likely to become alcoholics when adopted into nonalcoholic families than children whose natural parents were nonalcoholics. The old argument that alcoholics have underlying psychological or emotional disturbances (the so-called alcoholic personality) was debunked in these studies by the finding that adopted children whose natural parents included one or more alcoholics were no more likely to have a psychiatric disturbance than adopted children whose natural parents were nonalcoholics. Subsequent adoption studies confirmed Goodwin's work.

Research pioneered by Henri Begleiter and colleagues at the State University of New York Health Science Center in Brooklyn in the late 1970s added further weight to the genetic argument. Begleiter compared sons of alcoholics, age seven to thirteen, with sons of nonalcoholics (neither group of children had ever been exposed to alcohol or other drugs) and found that a specific type of electrical activity that occurs in the brain in response to certain sensory stimuli (and which is measured by the amplitude of the P3 brain wave) was markedly reduced in the children of alcoholics. These electrophysiological marker studies suggest, in Begleiter's words, "that decrements in P3 activity are not a consequence of years of heavy drinking but are genetic antecedents of alcohol abuse."

These are just a few of several dozen studies confirming that alcoholism is one of the more than three thousand known genetically influenced diseases in the human population caused by variations in DNA and passed down from one generation to the next. Given the fact that human beings have more than a hundred thousand genes, Blum knew that he was in for a long and difficult search.

> *The offspring of the alcohol-loving rodents inherit this fondness for booze, while the offspring of the alcohol-hating mice simply don't like the stuff.*

In January 1988 Blum called his friend and fellow researcher Ernest Noble, former director of the National Institute on Alcoholism and Alcohol Abuse. Now at the University of California, Los Angeles, conducting research on the brain electrophysiology of alcoholic fathers and their sons, Noble had access to a large collection of brains of deceased alcoholics and nonalcoholics, along with complete medical records. The alcoholic brains would be a perfect DNA source for Blum's experiment, Noble said, because they belonged to late-stage alcoholics who had experienced multiple relapses and died from alcohol-related pathologies. If there was indeed a genetic mutation causing alcoholism, these brains would have it.

Using more than fifty gene probes that allowed them to search inside the DNA, Blum and Noble looked for unusual or mutated genes associated with alcoholism. After a year, they were getting discouraged—the probes they were using were not able to penetrate the one area they suspected was directly linked to alcohol addiction: the genes controlling the actions of the neurotransmitter dopamine.

The A1 allele

In July 1989 Blum read an article in the *Wall Street Journal* about a successful cloning of the human D2 receptor (DRD^2) gene on chromosome 11. With great excitement he called the lead researcher, Olivier Civelli at Oregon Health Sciences University in Portland; Civelli said he would be happy to send Blum the D2 gene probe.

Using Civelli's probe, Blum and Noble renewed their quest for the abnormal genes. What they discovered in 1990 took their collective breath away. In the q22–q23 region of chromosome 11, they found a genetic mutation, which they later dubbed the A1 allele. Sixty-nine percent of the alcoholic brains in their sample contained the A1 allele, while 80 percent of the nonalcoholic brain tissue did not. In other words, looking only at this one genetic variation in brain tissue, the researchers could predict with 75 percent accuracy whether the brain belonged to an alcoholic or a nonalcoholic.

Blum's and Noble's research teams knew they had discovered only one of the genes associated with alcoholism, for 31 percent of the alcoholic brains did not contain the genetic abnormality. The challenge now facing Blum was to find the additional genes involved and eventually map out their actions and potentials.

The stunning discovery in 1990 of a gene mutation associated with alcoholism provides an avenue of fertile investigation into the potential biochemical, neurophysiological, and genetic roots of alcoholism. Researchers haven't mapped out all the genes involved, nor do they know the precise pattern of genes that combine to create varying degrees of susceptibility to alcoholism. They do know, however, that certain genes or gene combinations determine whether or not a specific individual will be predisposed to the disease of alcoholism.

Alcoholism Is Not a Disease

Edward A. Dreyfus

Edward A. Dreyfus is a clinical psychologist in private practice in the Los Angeles/Santa Monica area of California.

Many types of compulsive behavior, including alcoholism, are incorrectly viewed as diseases. Alcoholism was originally termed a disease in order to help people understand that it is a serious problem for which they should seek help. However, the disease model has been overused and distorted to the extent that many alcoholics and other emotionally disturbed people incorrectly believe that they are physically "sick" and need medical rather than psychological help to overcome their addictions.

M any mental health practitioners are promoting the notion that alcohol abuse, drug abuse, over-eating, gambling, anorexia, bulimia and smoking are diseases. By using the disease model, its proponents believe that people are more apt to seek help because having an "illness" is more acceptable than having psychological or behavior disorder. I am reminded of the effects of saying that people with emotional difficulties were "sick," and suffering from a "disease." Psychology and psychiatry moved a long way forward when we listened to Thomas Szasz declare that mental illness was a myth, to Karl Menninger discussing degrees of personality organization, and to Benjamin Rush when he spoke of problems in living. Now it appears we are moving backwards. What will be the next "disease" to appear in the news media?

The disease model states that alcoholism and compulsive over-eating, for example, are diseases and can be compared to diabetes in that diabetics react to sugar in a similar way that over-eaters have a reaction to food and alcoholics to liquor. Therefore, in both instances the individuals must carefully monitor their intake. If they do not rigidly adhere to their respective diets there will be dire consequences. The compulsive over-eater, for example, maintains that if he/she does not monitor food intake, there is a chemical imbalance which takes over and control over one's eating is no longer possible. So, the theory maintains, the compulsive over-eater is not "normal" insofar as eating is concerned, but rather he or she has a "disease" and is "sick."

The question that this thesis does not address, however, is: Why do compulsive over-eaters and alcoholics, knowing that they are not able to control their substance abuse once it is started, persist in breaking their diet? The diabetic's disease is the failure of the body to produce sufficient insulin; the disease is not the individual's failure to stay on a diabetic diet. It is not the *behavior* that is the disease, it is the manner in which the body metabolizes alcohol that may be the disease, leading to the necessity for dietary control, or in the case of the substance abuser and alcoholic, abstinence. While there may be a biological or chemical basis for some compulsions, the disease model does not account for the compulsive *behavior* itself; it only accounts for the specific substance.

Historical perspective

Many years ago mentally disturbed persons were considered to be inhabited by the devil; they were ostracized from their communities and families and were treated with disdain. They were locked up, deprived of their human rights, and often killed. Pinel, in the 18th century, cut the chains of the inmates of the insane asylum at Bicitre and freed them, declaring that they were not possessed of evil spirits, but rather that they were medically ill. This was the beginning of a movement which sought to achieve humane treatment for the mentally disturbed. It was an extremely important step forward. By declaring these people ill, the indignities they suffered were reduced. It was *necessary* to call them "sick" in order to obtain humane treatment.

It is pitiful that a society has to resort to seeing people as sick in order to be compassionate towards them.

As the theories of Sigmund Freud were made available and became acceptable, it was discovered that many of these individuals were not ill in the medical sense, but rather they were psychologically disturbed. The "talking cure," as psychoanalysis was then called, demonstrated that mental "illness" could be cured through words. This was another very important step, for now, people with psychological disorders could be viewed with some dignity and could potentially be treated by nonmedical practitioners. Unfortunately neither the patients nor the practitioners were accorded the same respect as those with physical ailments who were being treated by physicians. In fact, many people still believe it is much more acceptable to be physically ill than it is to be psychologically disturbed.

So, instead of being chained in dungeons and forgotten, the mentally ill were locked in hospitals and treated. However, it gradually became obvious that they were still ostracized from the community, and were being treated as second class citizens. Though they were treated better physically, they still carried the stigma of being "sick," which was almost as dehumanizing as being thought of as "inhabited by the devil." Now they were pitied, but they still lost their freedom, their dignity, and their human rights.

The movement away from the disease model towards a psychological model helped pave the way toward integrating the "mentally ill" into the community rather than segregating them. It had the effect of gaining more respect, understanding, and dignity for all people with emotional difficulties. Instead of seeing these people as "sick", we began seeing them as having "problems in living," which could be understood and resolved. Such a psychological model permitted greater numbers of non-medical practitioners to "treat" these individuals and has made such treatment more available and more affordable to more people. People began to feel more comfortable treating troubled people humanly without having to see them as "sick." (In fact, they found that the disease model interfered with effective treatment.) People trying to cope with internal or external stress may do so in maladaptive ways. This does not make them "sick."

Consequences of a disease model

When it came to compulsive behaviors, however, even the most compassionate individuals had difficulty accepting that people did not seem able to control their own behavior. Hence, they treated alcoholics as "bums," over-eaters as "fatsos," gamblers as "stupid," etc. And these people viewed themselves similarly. So, the concept of illness was invoked once again. And once again people were treated for their "illness" and others viewed them more compassionately as, "Don't laugh at your overweight Aunt Mary, she has an illness," or "Your drunk Uncle Charley is sick." I think it is pitiful that a society has to resort to seeing people as sick in order to be compassionate towards them. And I believe it adversely affects people's self-esteem to have to consider themselves sick in order to be related to humanly. I find it sad that people, so hungry for acceptance, both self-acceptance or acceptance from others, will accept the appellation "sick."

The advocates for various self-help and other groups that deal with compulsive substance abuse view these compulsions as diseases. They promote the concept of disease in order to entice substance abusers into treatment. If they can convince these people that they are "sick" and they are suffering from a "disease" then it is believed that more people will accept treatment.

We live in a society that loves labels whether on clothes or on people. We tend to relate to the clothes people, with the labels on the outside, just as we treat the labels we pin on people: schizophrenic, alcoholic, ACA [adult child of an alcoholic], incest survivor, borderline personality, etc. And people seem to need to view themselves as "sick" in order to be treated humanly (and in order to treat themselves with care.)

Using the disease concept, any one of us could be viewed as "sick" for any behavior that people deem compulsive.

Psychology strove for years to move away from the medical/disease model so that healers would relate to people as people, not as labels, not as "sick." This was called the humanistic movement and eschewed the medical model and sought a psychological model. I see a reversal of this effort and find it regressive. And I think, in this context, that 12-step programs with their emphasis on disease and "sickness," foster this regressive type of thinking.

While I do not object to the results or even some of the methods employed, I do object to the use of the terms "disease" and "sick" as a means for effecting these results. There are consequences to using a disease model which extend beyond merely controlling substance abuse. In our quest for expediency, we are often short-sighted.

Social consequences

I object to the idea that compulsive *behavior* is a disease. It does not matter whether there is a chemical imbalance that leaves these people vulnerable to gaining weight and drinking, the disease concept is not appropriate for the compulsive behaviors. Society decides on what is compulsive, and using the disease concept, any one of us could be viewed as "sick" for any behavior that people deem compulsive. Thus someone who is a "workaholic," a smoker, or a nail-biter could be considered "sick." Don't people have the right to engage in activities, even unhealthy activities, without being considered "sick"?

Compulsive behavior is rewarded in our society. Indeed, people are taught to be compulsive; that is, we are taught to be punctual, orderly, committed, organized, etc. We are taught to hide our feelings through activity. We are taught to keep busy when we are feeling badly. We are taught to whistle when afraid, think about something else when we are sad, and even to eat when we are "blue." All compulsive individuals are taught at an early age to deny feelings through some form of activity. And if you learn your lessons well, you could be considered "sick."

Psychological consequences

Some psychological consequences of the disease model are:
1. Individuals tend to give up responsibility for their life; they can see themselves as victims because the "disease" is not their fault.
2. Individuals seek someone to "fix" them without examining the causes or issues which may produce the compulsion; only the symptom is examined.
3. There is a loss of dignity and self-esteem in believing that one is "bad" or "sick" for having gone off a diet, or drinking, etc.
4. Individuals often use "illness" or "disease" to avoid taking responsibility for their behavior just as they might have gotten "sick" to avoid going to school.
5. This kind of infantilization has long-term consequences to one's self-esteem and self-confidence, though it may have immediate results. Patronizing others does not enhance one's self-concept.
6. By seeing oneself as "sick," one invites compassion and pity; and one then begins to see oneself as pitiful, hoping for a magical cure that someday will be discovered if one is "good."

Because we live in a society that also looks askew at individuals with psychological problems, especially compulsive disorders (they tend to be viewed as lacking in will-power or lacking in moral fiber), it is much more palatable to talk in terms of the "disease" which needs to be treated than it is to deal with maladaptive coping behaviors. It is more acceptable to go to the medical doctor's office than it is to go to the psychotherapist's office. So the disease model has much more appeal for the majority of our society.

Thus, what started out as a humane approach to a problem has become in itself a problem. Originally, calling compulsive behaviors a disease was for the purpose of increasing compassion toward the obese, the alcoholic, or the gambler. Gradually the solution has produced the very effect it sought to eliminate—namely, reducing human dignity and reinforcing the notion that one is not a responsible adult. Rather, the compulsive substance abuser is viewed as a helpless child who is "sick" and needs to be told what to do. (In fact, in some of these self-help programs, members are referred to as "babies.")

The "disease model" was only a metaphor *used to encourage people to seek help.*

There is no doubt that were we to promote a psychological model of abuse rather than a disease model, many individuals would not seek treatment; that would be their choice. However, in my opinion, there is greater harm to many more people from the potential loss of responsibility, choice, and dignity by invoking a disease model. What will be the next "sickness" for which treatment will be given? When do we have the right to behave differently than society dictates without being labeled "sick"?

Political consequences

If we accept a "disease" model for compulsive behavior, then what will stop people from thinking about other psychological disorders as disease? And if this happens, we will be back where we were 50 years ago, believing that all people with emotional problems are "sick." Who will treat these "sick" people? Clearly the medical profession has a vested interest in promoting a disease model, for it is physicians who treat the "sick." It does not matter to the public that the "disease model" was only a *metaphor* used to encourage people to seek help. Over time the metaphor is lost and we are left with a model that is inappropriate. While the idea of using a disease model as a metaphor, to make it more palatable for some people to accept treatment, has some short range appeal, the long range consequences may be less attractive.

Many people do not comprehend the use of the disease model as a metaphor or as a theoretical model for generating hypotheses. Metaphors and models often become functionally autonomous; they take on a reality of their own. Yesterday's metaphors become today's reality. As the use of the term "disease" increases, and with more public acceptance of the notion that compulsive behaviors are diseases, we must become concerned with the long term consequences on our thinking about the relationship between emotional disorders and disease.

Are we heading toward a time when, once again, people with problems in living and emotionally disturbed human beings will be viewed as "sick" and in need of medical, not psychological, treatment?

An alternative model

I think that a model based on integrating psychological, biological, and social factors for understanding and treating chemical dependency, addictions, and compulsive behaviors is more appropriate than a disease model. Such a model takes into account biological (including genetics, physiological predisposition, and chemical components), social, and psychological factors in understanding compulsive behaviors without invoking "sickness" or disease as causative. The individual, in this model, remains responsible for how s/he deals with their life without the loss in dignity.

This model accepts that there may be genetic, chemical, biological, etc. factors involved in some addictions (for not being able to metabolize alcohol, for example), but this does not account for why an individual continues to rely upon their addiction for dealing with problems in living. It recognizes that there are social issues involved in compulsive behavior which have nothing to do with biology or chemistry. It further states that psychological, not medical, factors are the most powerful in understanding and controlling human behavior. It accepts the basic principle that human beings are fundamentally responsible for their own behavior and have the power to choose how they will conduct their lives. It accepts that people are free to choose how they will live their life; even if that choice is self-destructive, it is still their choice. People can choose to play the game of life differently than most without being labeled "sick." They must, however, accept full responsibility for the consequences of that behavior.

3

Alcoholics Anonymous Is the Best Treatment for Alcoholics

Thomas Curtis Chace

Thomas Curtis Chace is the author of Am I? Am I Not? An Alcoholic. *He is a certified alcohol and drug counselor and has taught courses on AA's twelve steps of recovery at Santa Barbara City College's (SBCC) Continuing Education program.*

Alcoholics Anonymous (AA) is by far the most successful program for recovering alcoholics. AA is an association of men and women who come together to share their experiences and draw support from one another. AA is a completely self-supporting organization, accepting no money from the city, state, or federal governments. AA is not affiliated with any particular church denomination or sect. The only thing AA asks of its members is that they have a desire to stop drinking. AA is about alcoholics helping other alcoholics achieve sobriety—nothing more, nothing less.

The most successful program for the recovery from alcoholism is Alcoholics Anonymous. There is no second place. Nothing even comes close.

To introduce you to AA, and to help dispel the normal fears that we know you have—that all have—about going to AA and attending those *meetings,* let's talk about AA as it talks about itself. Shown below is what is known as "The Preamble." It says exactly what AA is all about and what it is not about. No matter what you've heard, no matter what you've read elsewhere, this is it. Nothing more. Nothing less. This is AA:

The AA Preamble

Alcoholics Anonymous is a fellowship of men and women who share their experience, strength and hope with each other that they may solve their common problem and help others to recover from alcoholism.

The only requirement for membership is a desire to stop

drinking. There are no dues or fees for AA membership; we are self-supporting through our own contributions. AA is not allied with any sect, denomination, politics, organization or institution; does not wish to engage in any controversy; neither endorses nor opposes any causes. Our primary purpose is to stay sober and help other alcoholics to achieve sobriety. *(Copyright © by the AA Grapevine, Inc.; reprinted with permission. Permission to reprint the AA Grapevine, Inc. copyrighted material does not in any way imply affiliation with or endorsement of any of the material contained in this publication.)*

"Alcoholics Anonymous is a fellowship of men and women. . . ." That is the beginning of the preamble of this miraculous organization that, without fanfare or fee, has literally saved the physical, emotional and mental health and lives of tens of thousands of problem drinkers. In those first few words are the heart of what AA is all about.

AA is a fellowship in the best sense of the word—it is companions with a common interest; friends sharing experiences and feelings; a group with one common problem and one common goal: to learn how to live, singly and collectively, in what seems to be a complex, often unfriendly, usually unfair and, certainly, unkind world without alcohol.

Never in AA are there lectures—or lecturers—or experts who cram something down dry throats.

That opening line also says a lot about what AA is not but is often accused of being by the misinformed. AA is not a cult, women's lib group, religious denomination, men's stag, school for learning to drink with honor, Skid Row hangout, Salvation Army house, left- or right-wing subversive bunch out to get boozers and those who make it or sell it. AA is a group of individuals—that's all it is.

AA is open to all men and women (including boys and girls) without much limit on age, and with no limit on social status, race, income, creed, length of drinking, how much drunk, religion, marital status, origin of birth, product drunk, sexual preference, color of hair or skin, et al.

AA is probably the first—maybe only—truly integrated, non-segregated, mix-em-up-and-pour-em-out group in the world. If you have a drinking problem, they don't care who you are, where you came from, what your name is, how much money you have, who you work for or any of those things that make you a name and number elsewhere. If you drink too much at the wrong times and it gets you into trouble—any trouble—at home, work or play, then you belong in AA. That's what it says: you're welcome, regardless.

The Preamble goes on: ". . . who share their experience, strength and hope with each other that they may solve their common problem and help others to recover from alcoholism." The key here is sharing, the realization that you are not alone, that others—thousands of others—feel as you do.

Through sharing their experiences of drinking, what happened to bring about a desire for change and their experiences of gaining sobriety, members of AA can identify with each other and learn from each other.

Never in AA are there lectures—or lecturers—or experts who cram something down dry throats. There are no professionals, no leaders, no teachers other than the members themselves who have been there and done that. Every bad story can be topped; every sad story empathized with; every failure matched; every success emulated. In AA they share, not dare.

Their experiences come from living, drunk and sober. If one can do it, so can all. In that concept, that simple idea, lies the hope of recovery. How many times do we hear, "If he can make it with all his problems, so can I."

Thus it is with sobriety in AA.

Working together

Members of AA are like trees in a forest all reaching for the sun, each with its own roots, supported and protected by others, some older, some stronger. All came from the same ground and from similar seeds or acorns. They grow together, not getting in each other's way, but sharing in fresh breezes, revitalizing rains and nurturing from the same soil. At times they hold each other up, encouraging growth while discouraging rampaging storms of destruction that would topple young saplings. They protect through their common strength those getting started and those who falter.

It is with the hope of their own recovery that fellow members of AA reach out for those still suffering. In helping them, they help themselves, for they are never cured, but always recovering. As others come in and begin, old-timers learn from the newcomers and remember the hell they suffered so they don't have to go out and do it again. They all share. They all contribute, newcomer and old-timer. It is from that sharing, one on one or one to the group, that comes the hope and ability to solve the common problem and help others to recover from the common problem, alcoholism.

No obligations

"The only requirement for membership is a desire to stop drinking," the Preamble continues. Nothing mystic! No fraternal gobbledygook. No psychobabble. No initiation fee. No nominating committee. No screening board. Not even an application. All you need to join AA is a *desire* to stop drinking. It's not even a requirement that you *must* stop. Thousands have come to AA drunk and continue to drink for months while they attend meetings. That's okay with AA. Keep coming back!

Encouraged to keep coming back, most eventually make it and their desire becomes a reality. If you want what they have, a comfortable sobriety, AA says you can get it regardless of your present condition or circumstances. All you need to start in the fellowship is "a desire to stop drinking." The first edition of the Preamble said, "an *honest* desire." The word honest was eventually dropped. The only requirement today is to want to quit, to have a simple desire to want to stop.

Maybe that desire will change after a few meetings and you no longer want what AA has to offer. That's okay. The door swings both ways. You are free to come and go as that desire carries you. As there is no initiation fee, there also is no refund. As the saying goes, they'll gladly give back your misery and wish you well on your journey back.

"There are no dues or fees for AA membership; we are self-supporting through our own contributions." Can you believe that? Ever hear of an organization that doesn't want your money? Your church, club, union, United Way, apartment association, YMCA? To belong you have to pay, right? Not in AA. There are no dues—period. There are no fees—period. AA takes from no one on the outside. It is self-supporting!

Because AA has no professionals, it has no salaries. Most meetings have to pay rent. They generally have coffee and cake to buy. That is handled by passing a basket. Most members put in a buck or two. That's it. No records are kept, no roll-call taken, no attendance reports written, no lists published of who paid and who owes or who was there and who was not.

Most meetings end the month with a small surplus from the baskets. What's left over generally goes to the area's Central Committee. The activities of this sub-group, usually made up of volunteers, is supported entirely by contributions from the meetings/groups, that is, by the members through the baskets.

The Central Committee usually provides the twenty-four-hour telephone answering service, a clearing house for literature and a drop-in center for those with questions or problems about the disease of alcoholism. The secretary or executive director of the Central Office may or may not be paid a salary (usually part-time, part-pay). Such expenses are covered by whatever the individual meeting groups send in. No one tells any meeting or member how much.

Loose and very tenuous. Somehow it works—or it has since 1935, when AA was first formed.

[AA members] are never cured, but always recovering.

To amplify on this highly unusual financial condition, one of AA's traditions . . . states that "Every AA group ought to be fully self-supporting, declining outside contributions." This means that no individual, group, foundation, trust, will or private enterprise can give money to AA.

You know that those of means, or their families who have successfully recovered from alcoholism and been given years of productive, happy, sober and profitable lives would love to give or leave something to the source of their well-being. Hard as it may be to grasp, their benevolence is turned away. Outside money and large individual gifts are simply not accepted. AA is truly self-supporting through the contributions of the current, active members.

AA has never taken, nor will it ever take, one cent of any government support. Not from the city. Not from the county, state or federal sources. Not a grant or a gift. Not a tax receiver is AA. It is self-supporting—always has been and always will be, now and forever. The individual groups have never asked for or been granted any special tax favors. AA gives and does not take.

No religious affiliation

"AA is not allied with any sect, denomination, politics, organization or institution; does not wish to engage in any controversy; neither endorses nor opposes any causes." Now there's a statement that sets AA aside from all others. AA is an organization with over four million members worldwide. Yet AA—as a local body, through the National General Service Office, or through any individual members—takes no position on anything. This applies to legislation even when it has to do with the beverage industry, drunk driving, state funds for alcoholism rehabilitation, teenage drinking, cleaning up Skid Row or supporting one of their own members for public office.

AA is not a religion.

People in AA talk openly about God in their meetings. They let it be known that AA is not a religion; not Jewish, Christian or Holy whatsoever, although many formalized churches and denominations endorse the AA program and send their members there for help.

AA doesn't have its own hospital or rehab-houses. Nor does it recommend one over another or even suggest they are beneficial or unnecessary in the treatment of alcoholism. Unlike most successful organizations, AA does not have a line of promotional materials for sale from which it receives a commission. In this day of all kinds of people promoting all kinds of things, can you believe that AA has not cashed in on the marketplace? Better believe it!

AA does not sell or lend its name to anyone or anything, regardless of how wonderful it or its work or aspirations may be. There is no official AA anything! AA does not endorse anyone or anything. Nor does it criticize anyone or anything. AA is free and independent of personal or political pressure, which is one of the main reasons it is successful. It is beholden to no one.

AA's sole purpose is sobriety

Because the sole and distinct purpose of AA is to help others into recovery from alcoholism, it does not get involved in any way in any project, program or political undertaking—no matter how wonderful and how tempting. AA truly minds its own business. The members continually remind themselves that when they speak, as individuals, it is only their opinions being expressed and not those of AA.

The Preamble ends, "Our primary purpose is to stay sober and help other alcoholics to achieve sobriety." The two go together. As one alcoholic helps another—even if one is drunk—the act of helping contributes another day to the life of the sober one. This, then, is the key to AA sobriety: a dry drunk helping a wet one: Bill W., co-founder of AA seeking out Dr. Bob, the other co-founder, in 1935; the newcomer being warmly welcomed into an AA group a half-century later.

"In order to keep it," the saying goes, "we must give it away," one drunk helping another. One sober alcoholic is able to stay sober only by seeking out another suffering alcoholic and helping him or her through his or her experience, strength and hope of achieving sobriety through the fellowship of Alcoholics Anonymous.

We hope by now that AA has lost some of its mystery. We suggest attending an open meeting of Alcoholics Anonymous, where anyone is welcome be they alcoholic or not. Here's an even better idea: Let someone in your hometown pick you up and drive you to a local meeting tonight, in your community, in your neighborhood.

All it takes is your telephone call to your local AA Central Office or group. They are listed in your local telephone directory white pages under Alcoholics Anonymous or AA. Why not do it right now? We'll wait.

The meeting will be relaxed, open and fun. You don't have to say anything or do anything. You don't even have to have a cup of coffee or give your name. If you have never been to an AA meeting, you're in for a surprise.

4

Alcoholics Anonymous Is Not the Best Treatment for Alcoholics

Jack Trimpey

Jack Trimpey is the founder of Rational Recovery, a network of self-help groups. He is also the author of The Small Book *and* Rational Recovery: The New Cure for Substance Addiction.

Alcoholics Anonymous (AA) does not believe in helping people recover from their addictions. Instead, AA seeks to impose its will upon addicted people. AA defeats the First Amendment by forcing a religion down the throats of alcohol abusers. AA is not about helping addicts recover from addictions; AA is a cult that values its unity above any individual. In preaching its religion of "twelve steps," AA diverts millions of people away from the most obvious and significant focus of recovery: abstinence from alcohol and drugs.

Alcoholics Anonymous (AA) is an American icon, the great hope of mainstream society that mass addiction will subside. AA is seemingly immune to criticism and public scrutiny. Very few people, including public officials who actively support the AA cartel, have actually read AA doctrinal literature, or even the list of the Twelve Steps, which are obviously religious. Even fewer have sat down in a typical meeting of the recovery group movement, to observe the indoctrination of newcomers into the ideology of powerlessness, helplessness, and dependence. AA sows the seeds of addiction before itself, then poses as a solution as it advances. AA shows the friendly side of tyranny, fronting honorable values to the public and media, while imposing its will upon addicted people behind closed doors. Their methods of indoctrination are an offense to common decency, with the result that many pay tribute to AA even while their own addictions progress toward despair and death. AA has found a niche in the dark side of the human psyche, and made it into a lair from which it preys on human vulnerabilities.

From "Why It Is Good to Speak Out Against AA," by Jack Trimpey, *The Real AA: Behind the Myth of 12-Step Recovery*, edited by Ken Ragge (Tucson, AZ: See Sharp Press, 1998). Copyright © 1998 by Ken Ragge. Reprinted by permission of the author.

Reasons to speak out against AA

1. By speaking out against AA, you will warn others to stay away from recovery groups of all kinds, and thus prevent harm to addicted people. Recovery groups create an illusion of hope during desperate times. You will also be encouraging addicted people that they can do the obvious—quit their addictions once and for all, rather than adopt the foolishness of abstaining one-day-at-a-time. Most addicted people recover on their own, and we must expect and encourage them to do so. AA doesn't believe in people at all. They believe in AA. When people improve, they must praise AA and never take credit themselves. America must start believing in people, not programs, so that addicted people may finally shoulder a burden that no society can—the burden of self-recovery from substance addictions.

There is no treatment, medical or otherwise, for addiction, for there is no disease.

By speaking out against AA, you will put the helping professions, particularly medicine, on notice that they have already committed a grave offense against the society they were sanctioned to protect. They have accepted money to perform services they are not qualified to perform. There is no treatment, medical or otherwise, for addiction, for there is no disease. This was well-known among the professions until rivers of tax dollars gushed forth, and those who were licensed to bill—stole. The professionals may eventually be forgiven for this ethical catastrophe, but not until they have admitted they were wrong.

2. If you love your country, speak out against AA. America is a unique society in human history, built on values of individualism, self-reliance, moral virtues, personal liberty, justice, and religious freedom. What appears to be a fellowship of recovered people offering encouragement to addicted people is actually the drug culture of America between their own drinking and using episodes. These are not the kind of people from whom to seek help of any kind. They are not recovered from their own addictions, and admit this freely. They have abandoned their own family values for the ersatz religion of AA. They have renamed the ultimate self-indulgence, addiction, a "disease," and accordingly do not know right from wrong. The group norms are sharply at odds with religious values, moral intuitions, and traditional mental health concepts.

People are arrested for alcohol or drug use, convicted of a crime, and are then required to profess that they are not responsible for their own actions. They are provided a doctor's excuse for their illegal behavior after their convictions. This corruption of justice is eating at the fabric of our society. Most people recognize that something is wrong with America, that we are becoming a nation of victims dependent on an ever-expanding array of government services. The engine of this disturbance is the 12-step recovery group movement, which proselytizes its mentality of victimhood and entitlement via government decree and popular media. By speaking out against AA, you can stop our progress toward becoming a therapeutic state, in which prisons and hospitals are one and the same.

The religion of AA

3. If you are a religious person, it is good to speak out against AA. The keystone of American society is the separation of organized religion from government affairs. AA has defeated the First Amendment of the U.S. Constitution and become our state religion. We can't stop this from happening; it has already happened. No one spoke out against Alcoholics Anonymous.

AA is bad religion. It is a Gnostic heresy, easily recognizable as such by any trained theologian. AA teaches addicted people to expect miracles on demand, a juvenile attitude discouraged by legitimate religions. Its homogenized deity can be a toad, but this idolatry is ignored by clergy who have been taught that addiction is a disease and idolatry is treatment. AA stole the sin of addiction from the churches of America and made it into a disease which no physician can treat or cure. In sharp contrast to any of the world's great religions, which view abstinence or temperance as a way to find or to honor God, AA poses God as an obstacle to the moral act of recovery through planned abstinence. The AA deity must be worshipped as a condition for abstinence from alcohol and drugs. Legitimate religious charities never hold back bread on condition of religious conversion. They give freely, expecting no tribute or submission, and welcome those who, once fed, enter freely into the faith. AA threatens addicted people with death unless they come to believe the AA creed. They use our courts, prisons, and social institutions to enforce their rule over desperate, addicted people. This is exactly what our Founding Fathers most feared—that America would succumb to the tendency of nations to impose religion upon its citizens.

Why didn't organized religion speak out, as AA grew in membership and might? Some didn't criticize AA because they were afraid of AA, afraid they would be criticized for criticizing. That is how all tyrannies gain power. But others didn't criticize AA because they thought they saw another religion. Interdenominational disputes are rare in the land of the free, and AA has been granted a shield against criticism which is common etiquette among religions. But AA is powerful, cunning, and baffling. It denies it is religious—only "spiritual." This way, it has infiltrated our public institutions, where it now paves the way for itself.

AA threatens addicted people with death unless they come to believe the AA creed.

The United States, with the worst track record managing substance abuse of all nations, exports a product far more dangerous than narcotics or other drugs. We export AA to other nations which have always had adequate means to manage substance abuse. Those nations will copy our errors, and succumb to mass addiction. AA ambassadors preach disease hysteria, announcing grave consequences unless those governments employ its members at new AA treatment centers. AA seeks a new world order based on God-control of all nations. Books have been written depicting AA founder, Bill W., as the reincarnated Christ. AA is a dangerous cult risen to power, which seeks world domination. Churches must unite to resist AA, using their legitimate moral authority.

AA is misleading

4. If you are an addicted person, it is good to speak out against AA because you have been misled about the nature of addiction and the nature of recovery. There is not a word or suggestion in the 12-step program concerning planned abstinence. To the contrary, newcomers are immediately informed that they are powerless to immediately and independently quit their addictions. Instead of directing seriously addicted people toward this direct, powerful, life-saving action, groupers routinely distract newcomers from this direct, powerful decision by drawing them into disorienting discussions of metaphysics, pop-psychology, and AA lore.

Books have been written depicting AA founder, Bill W., as the reincarnated Christ.

Anyone can quit an addiction if they want to and know what they are doing. AA is not about addictions or abstinence; AA is about AA. The recovery group movement diverts millions of people away from the most obvious and significant focus of recovery—abstinence from alcohol and drugs. If you criticize AA, you will discover that you have no friends in AA but only partners in the fellowship. AA is a cult which values its unity above any individual, and its members believe their survival depends on the truth of its doctrine. If you criticize AA, you also threaten them, and they will cut you loose with a grim prediction—a jinx—that you will self-destruct by drinking. It's good to know who your friends are. If you were required to attend AA by force, professional intimidation, court mandate, or by lack of information about other means to recover, your rights were certainly abused, including your Constitutional rights. As you criticize AA, you will feel stronger and you will see more clearly that the 12-step program fits over an addiction perfectly. In truth, the 12-step program is the philosophy of addiction itself, wrapped up in God-talk to fool the larger society. When you see this, you will know better that you were on the right track while struggling alone, and that it is not you, but the groupers, who are crazy.

The AA cartel exists solely because people do not criticize AA. If we don't raise our voices now, mass addiction will grow worse, more billions of your tax dollars will be wasted, liberty and freedom be further limited, and it will become more difficult to throw the rascals out of our public institutions. Don't be fooled by people who say AA shouldn't be criticized because it has helped so many people. AA has helped no one, failed millions, fooled most everyone, and taken credit for the success of a few of its members who have stopped drinking. Speak up for your rights! Help people recover from addictions! Help your country! Be true to your religious faith! It is good to speak out against Alcoholics Anonymous and the recovery group movement!

5

Alcoholics Cannot Learn to Drink in Moderation

Mike Harden

Mike Harden is a Columbus Dispatch *columnist.*

Audrey Kishline, a recovering alcoholic and the founder of Moderation Management, proposed that people with drinking problems could learn to control their drinking through moderation. Kishline believed that for many problem drinkers, moderate drinking was a more realistic goal than all-out abstinence. However, this view contradicts decades of experience showing that alcoholism is a disease that can only be cured with abstinence. In March 2000 Kishline killed a man and his 12-year old daughter during a drunk driving accident where her blood-alcohol level was .26, more than three times the legal limit. This tragedy demonstrates that alcoholics cannot learn to moderate their drinking.

Six years ago, the mere mention of author Audrey Kishline's book *Moderate Drinking* was enough to set the alcohol-treatment community on edge all the way from Manhattan to Maui.

"I met the lady and debated her on television before," said Dr. Tom Pepper, medical director of Talbot Hall, Ohio State University's alcohol and chemical dependency treatment center.

Kishline was a proponent of the notion that problem drinkers could teach themselves to drink socially once again by following her "nine steps toward moderation and balance."

Moderation Management

Her book, subtitled *The Moderation Management Guide for People Who Want To Reduce Their Drinking*, made her a much-sought-after subject for talk shows. *Psychology Today* showcased her controversial plan in a cover article that appeared after publication of *Moderate Drinking*. Kishline argued that self-imposed behavior modification techniques are sufficient to corral unmanaged drinking patterns. She said such techniques spare individuals the ordeal of treatment and lifelong consignment to an abstinence-based re-covery program.

"I don't know of any credible organization or publication that rec-ommends controlled drinking for people with alcoholic drinking pat-terns," Pepper said. "You can make a pickle out of a cucumber, but you can't make a cucumber out of a pickle. Controlled drinking is that at-tempt to unpickle the cucumber."

Kishline believed otherwise. She suggested that her personal experi-ences with the 12-step program of Alcoholics Anonymous had left her wanting for a less rigid way to address drinking issues. Promotional copy heralding publication of her book noted, "Based on her own unsatisfac-tory experience with abstinence-based programs, Kishline offers inspira-tion and a step-by-step program to help individuals avoid the kind of drinking that detrimentally affects their lives."

"Moderation management is nothing but alcoholics covering up their problem."

Her Web site for Moderation Management explained, "MM is in-tended for problem drinkers who have experienced mild-to-moderate lev-els of alcohol-related problems."

Jill Reese, a Talbot Hall staff member, has observed attempts to make social drinkers of people with significant alcohol-related problems. "I've worked in this field for 20 years, and I've never met anybody who could pull it off."

After basking in the talk-show limelight, Kishline faded from public controversy and—so it seemed—became less a thorn in the side of alcohol-treatment experts.

Moderation kills

Not many days ago [on June 20, 2000], however, she was the subject of a news release prepared by the National Council on Alcoholism and Drug Dependence. The release was issued on the day Kishline, 43, was sched-uled to go to trial on two counts of vehicular manslaughter in Washing-ton state.

According to police reports and news accounts, Kishline on March 25 [2000] was driving her pickup truck in the wrong direction on Washing-ton's I-90. She struck a vehicle driven by Richard Davis of Yakima County.

Davis was killed instantly. His 12-year-old daughter, LaSchell, died before reaching the hospital.

Kishline's blood-alcohol level was measured at 0.26 following the crash, a reading which—in Washington—is more than three times the le-gal limit. She was hospitalized briefly for chest and facial injuries.

Two months before the fatal crash, Kishline apparently had experienced second thoughts about her personal issues with alcohol. She announced on her Web site that she was stepping down as Moderation Management's spokeswoman and giving up moderation drinking for abstinence.

Kishline wept as she pleaded guilty on Thursday [June 29, 2000] to two counts of vehicular homicide in the deaths of Davis and his daughter. Kishline's lawyer told a Seattle journalist that his client is "extremely remorseful" and that she had carried photographs of the two crash victims with her at an alcohol treatment center.

Sources said Kishline conceded that "moderation management is nothing but alcoholics covering up their problem."

That admission doesn't come as news to Tom Pepper or Jill Reese any more than it does to the National Council on Alcoholism and Drug Dependence.

Would that the price of Kishline's awakening were consequences that only she had to deal with.

6

Alcoholics Can Learn to Drink in Moderation

Stanton Peele

Stanton Peele is a psychologist, researcher, and the author of Diseasing of America: How We Allowed Recovery Zealots and the Treatment Industry to Convince Us We Are Out of Control. *Peele has also published numerous articles in magazines and journals.*

Audrey Kishline, the founder of Moderation Management, made national headlines on March 25, 2000, when she killed a father and his daughter in a drunk-driving accident. Kishline believed that problem drinkers could return to levels of moderate drinking and promoted this idea through her alternative alcohol therapy program, Moderation Management (MM). Critics have seized the opportunity to use Kishline's accident as final proof that MM is a failure and that abstinence is the only solution. However, Kishline had left MM and rejoined Alcoholics Anonymous (AA) at the time of the accident. AA is not necessarily to blame for Kishline's accident, but neither is moderate drinking. Moreover, many studies indicate that moderate drinking can be a successful solution for some problem drinkers.

At 6 P.M. on March 25 [2000], Audrey Kishline was driving west on the eastbound side of Interstate 90 near Seattle when her Ford pickup truck collided head-on with a Dodge coupe occupied by Richard Davis, 38, and his 12-year-old daughter, LaSchell, killing both of them. Kishline had a half-empty vodka bottle on the seat beside her when police found her, unconscious, in her truck. Her blood-alcohol level was 0.26 percent, more than three times Washington's legal limit for drivers. Three months later, she pleaded guilty to two counts of vehicular homicide in Kittitas County Superior Court.

Spokesperson for moderation

The crash, however tragic and avoidable, would have been no more newsworthy than the thousands of other drunk driving accidents in which Americans are killed each year were it not for the fact that Kishline is the author of the 1994 book *Moderate Drinking* and founder of Moderation Management, an organization aimed at helping problem drinkers control their alcohol consumption. (I wrote an introduction to the book and served as an adviser to M.M.) To longtime critics of the "controlled drinking" Kishline espoused as an alternative to the abstinence urged by Alcoholics Anonymous and its imitators, the crash was a vindication. The National Council on Alcohol and Drug Dependence (NCADD)—a private group that, like A.A., considers alcoholism a disease that can be controlled only through abstinence—gloated in a press release that Kishline's crash taught a "harsh lesson for all of society, particularly those individuals who collude with the media to continually question abstinence-based treatment for problems related to alcohol and other drugs."

Yet Kishline's one brief statement to the press revealed some facts that ran counter to the NCADD's interpretation. "Two months before the crash," *The Seattle Times* reported, "she dropped out of the [M.M.] program and joined Alcoholics Anonymous. But it wasn't long before she was consuming so much wine at night she would drink herself to sleep." In other words, Kishline, who belonged to A.A. before founding M.M., had returned. Only then, it appears, did her drinking veer out of control.

Of course, it is as unfair to blame A.A. for the Kishline tragedy as it is to blame M.M. She was apparently experiencing family and financial difficulties that had thrown her life off kilter after seven years of moderate drinking. While M.M. attracted media attention, it had never provided a reliable source of income. Kishline's husband was an itinerant businessman, and she had moved with him four times in the previous seven years. They and their two young daughters ended up living with her in-laws in a small town outside Seattle. But whatever the circumstances of Kishline's relapse, it is a mark of ideological intransigence and intellectual dishonesty that critics such as the NCADD do not note that she was regularly attending A.A. at the time of the crash.

Kishline's story is not just a tale of personal despair and failure. It embodies centuries of American conflict over alcohol in which teetotalers have repeatedly clashed with advocates of moderation. Having failed to impose their vision on the rest of the nation through Prohibition, the forces of abstinence nowadays focus mainly on problem drinkers, insisting that they renounce alcohol rather than try to use it more responsibly. This stubborn position overlooks substantial evidence that the sort of moderation training once advocated by Kishline can succeed where abstinence fails.

Abstinence is not the only answer

The A.A.-style abstinence approach dominates American treatment programs. A 1997 survey of private treatment centers found that 93 percent followed A.A.'s 12 steps (which include admitting that one is "powerless over alcohol") and 99 percent insisted upon abstinence. The belief that alcoholics must abstain is so ensconced in American folklore that contrary research findings tend to produce angry responses.

In 1976, a RAND Corp. study found that 22 percent of alcoholics were drinking without problems 18 months following treatment, compared to 24 percent who were abstaining. Luther Cloud, board member of the National Council on Alcoholism (the NCADD's forerunner), claimed the RAND study would lead to "death and brain damage" among alcoholics. Yet in a four-year follow-up study, the RAND investigators found that many alcoholics continued to drink without problems. Indeed, for some categories of alcoholics, abstainers were at greater risk of relapse than moderate drinkers.

The belief that alcoholics must abstain is so ensconced in American folklore that contrary research findings tend to produce angry responses.

The RAND researchers simply reported on patients in federal alcohol treatment centers, all of which were abstinence-oriented. But in the early 1970s two psychologists, Mark and Linda Sobell, had published research showing that alcoholics they treated with moderation techniques fared better than alcoholics treated in a standard hospital abstinence program. In 1982 three researchers, led by psychologist Mary Pendery, published a rebuttal of the Sobells' work in the prestigious journal *Science,* charging that the Sobells had misreported their data and that subjects trained to drink moderately often relapsed. The Pendery group's accusations led to a series of investigations by the Canadian Addition Research Foundation, the U.S. Alcohol, Drug Abuse, and Mental Health Administration, and a congressional subcommittee, all of which exonerated the Sobells of wrongdoing. As a result of the investigations, the Sobells' finding that the abstinence-trained alcoholics had more relapses was actually reinforced.

In a disturbing postscript to this episode, Mary Pendery was shot to death in 1994 by an extremely intoxicated lover who had been treated by the hospital program where Pendery had worked. This incident, which on the face of it did not reflect well on the abstinence approach, did not get anything like the attention attracted by Kishline's crash, which was widely cited as evidence that alcoholics cannot learn to moderate their drinking and so must abstain. A closer look reveals a more complicated story.

Moderation Management

At 43, Audrey Kishline had had a drinking problem for years. After treatment with two inpatient alcohol programs, a series of counselors, and A.A., she concluded that there was a better way. In the summer of 1993, she contacted me and several other nontraditionalists in the alcoholism field for assistance in creating her own support group.

The psychologists whose work Kishline consulted contended that there were two groups of alcohol abusers: alcoholics who display the full array of symptoms, including tolerance and withdrawal, and less severely afflicted "problem drinkers," who encounter personal, family, social, work, or legal problems due to drinking. Moderation Management was explicitly presented as a support group for "problem drinkers" who wanted to reduce their drinking to safe levels (quite low ones of, at most, nine drinks weekly for women and 14 for men). In the aftermath of the RAND and Sobell controversies, it was only with such drinkers that behavioral psychologists would dare to attempt moderation therapy, since using that approach with drinkers identified as alcoholics would have invited intense professional criticism and raised the possibility of legal liability. Even so, such psychologists deviate significantly from the disease model, which holds that even a taste of booze sets off a craving in an alcoholic that inevitably leads to excess. Instead, they view problem drinking as a learned response to stressful situations and negative feelings.

Alcoholics vs. problem drinkers

You wouldn't think that traditional, 12-step alcoholism counselors would object to moderation for problem drinkers, since they themselves maintain that it is only *real* alcoholics who need to abstain. But this seeming agreement masks longstanding conflicts, because both sides say it is impossible to know for sure, before the fact, which drinkers need to abstain and which can learn to drink moderately. Thus when Sally Satel, an anti-disease-theory psychiatrist, defended moderation training in *The New York Times* after Kishline's guilty plea, she undermined her own argument by saying, "The distinction between the problem drinker and the alcoholic, while not razor sharp, exists." Since the line is hard to draw, 12-step advocates argue, therapists should err on the side of caution by urging everyone with a drinking problem to abstain.

> *Kishline's crash . . . was widely cited as evidence that alcoholics cannot learn to moderate their drinking. . . . A closer look reveals a more complicated story.*

When Caroline Knapp wrote about the Kishline case for *Salon*, she was certain that alcoholics can never moderate, because she had tried and failed. Knapp—author of *Drinking: A Love Story*, which details her alcoholic degradation and redemption through A.A.—cited no research to support her claim. But what was most remarkable was how similar her language was to Satel's. "If an individual has crossed the line, admittedly fuzzy, into alcoholism," Satel had written, "then the risks of allowing someone to have an occasional drink or two become too high." Knapp wrote, "The line between problem drinking and full-fledged alcoholism may be blurry and difficult to discern—certainly it's difficult for the drinker to accept—but once you've passed a certain point in your abuse, moderation simply ceases to be an option."

The problem drinker/alcoholic dichotomy is a vague approximation of reality. Although the American Psychiatric Association classifies alcohol disorders as either "alcohol abuse" (i.e., problem drinking) or "alcohol dependence," most investigators and clinicians (especially those outside the U.S.) prefer to place drinkers along a scale, based on a combination of social problems (e.g., arrests, fights) and medical symptoms (e.g., withdrawal-induced "shakes"). According to this incremental view, the more severely dependent the drinker, the less likely moderation is—at least without the passage of substantial time.

Even that formulation is overly reductive: Several teams of researchers in the United Kingdom, for example, have found that problem drinkers' beliefs—whether they see themselves as "powerless," for example, or whether they think a single drink will set off a relapse—influence whether abstinence or controlled drinking is the more attainable goal. In other words, the very subjective elements that American alcoholism treatment derides as "denial" can improve the chances of recovery: It is easier to achieve what you believe.

Problem drinkers' beliefs . . . influence whether abstinence or controlled drinking is the more attainable goal.

The point is not that moderation training is always better than abstinence. But even if abstinence was the right goal for Audrey Kishline, she didn't manage it. Therapists, whatever their orientation, are reluctant to admit that most alcohol abusers relapse, and that they need training to avoid harming themselves and others when they do. For example, people can learn in therapy to call their spouse when they get drunk to make sure they don't drive while intoxicated. By failing to develop such fallback positions, therapists and support groups are saying, in effect, "If you make a mistake, you might as well give up all restraint—taking a drink, getting drunk, and driving drunk are all equivalent."

When Kishline repopularized the idea that some people could return to nonproblematic drinking, she aroused the ire of the NCADD, which denounced the idea in a July 1995 press release. "Millions of Americans," it said, "have recently seen life-threatening stories in the media that people with alcohol problems don't have to stop drinking completely to get better." In perhaps the high point of national media attention Moderation Management was to receive, *U.S. News & World Report* featured controlled drinking and M.M. in a July 1997 cover story. The article focused on problem drinkers, who it indicated were a solid majority of those with alcohol problems. Nonetheless, the director of the government's National Institute on Alcohol Abuse and Alcoholism (NIAAA), Enoch Gordis, wrote a letter to the magazine emphasizing that "persons with the medical disorder 'alcohol dependence'" need to abstain.

The evidence supports controlled drinking

The NIAAA's own research has contradicted that position. Project MATCH was the largest trial of alcoholism treatment ever conducted. Completed in 1996, less than a fifth of the 952 alcoholics who underwent only outpatient treatment, and a little more than a third of the 774 alcoholics who had hospital treatment followed by outpatient treatment, abstained for as long as a year. So the NIAAA used a different standard of success: It emphasized that the subjects entered treatment drinking, on average, 25 days per month and 15 drinks per occasion; after treatment they drank, on average, five to six days a month and three drinks per occasion. The NIAAA in this case seemed to be endorsing controlled drinking.

In 1992 the NIAAA conducted face-to-face interviews with a representative sample of nearly 43,000 Americans, asking them about their current and past drinking practices. Of the more than 4,500 who had been alcohol dependent at some point in their lives according to the current psychiatric definition, about a quarter had entered treatment as a result. A third of those who had been treated were drinking abusively at the time of the survey, compared to a quarter of those who hadn't been treated. Untreated alcoholics were less likely to be abusing alcohol, but they were twice as likely to be drinking without qualifying as problem drinkers or alcoholics. Abstinence was more common among alcoholics who had been in treatment, but still only a minority (39 percent) were abstaining, while 28 percent were drinking without diagnosable problems. Those who had been treated did, on average, have worse problems to begin with. But all of the drinkers in the analysis had at one time qualified for the diagnosis of alcohol dependence and would certainly have been considered in need of treatment. A plausible explanation for the finding that treated alcoholics were more likely to be drinking abusively is the all-or-nothing message taught by A.A.-style programs: When people who have undergone traditional treatment fall off the wagon, they're convinced that it marks the beginning of a binge, which then becomes a self-fulfilling prophecy.

When people who have undergone traditional [abstinence-only] treatment fall off the wagon, they're convinced that it marks the beginning of a binge.

Thus, federal research whose size and comprehensiveness will not readily be equaled gives the lie to the principal claims of America's treatment establishment: that alcoholics can't recover without treatment; that alcoholics can't reduce their drinking to nonproblematic levels; and that alcoholism treatment reliably produces abstinence.

Ignoring this evidence, abstinence-only advocates are using the Kishline case to close the small cracks that have appeared in the 12-step monolith.

[In 2000], under medical director Alexander DeLuca, the Smithers Center in New York—founded by the late R. Brinkley Smithers, a wealthy recovering alcoholic and A.A. supporter—began to make referrals to M.M. DeLuca did not himself offer moderation treatment at Smithers. Rather, in keeping with the ethical and legal requirement of informed consent, he thought it proper to discuss alternatives such as controlled drinking with patients who were not fully committed to quitting. DeLuca still hoped such patients would ultimately decide to abstain.

Despite these nuances, in July 2000 the board of the Smithers Foundation, headed by Brinkley Smithers' widow, Adele Smithers-Fornaci, took out a full-page ad in *The New York Times* attacking the reconstituted Smithers program (with which her family is no longer associated). "The seductive appeal of controlled drinking to the alcoholic will cause needless loss of life and destruction of families," the ad warned. "This is no more sadly illustrated than in the tragically ironic case of the founder of the Moderation Management program, Audrey Kishline. . . . Using the Smithers name in conjunction with this type of treatment is an abomination, an insult and a disgrace to the memory of R. Brinkley Smithers." Within days of the ad's appearance, the Smithers Center accepted DeLuca's resignation.

7

Colleges Should Promote Tougher Policies Against Alcohol Abuse

Henry Wechsler, Toben Nelson, and Elissa R. Weitzman

Henry Wechsler, Toben Nelson, and Elissa R. Weitzman are researchers at the Harvard School of Public Health College Alcohol Study (CAS), an ongoing survey of college students.

Binge drinking is a severe problem facing most college campuses. Binge drinking contributes to an array of social problems, including overdoses, physical assaults, and unwanted sexual advances. Education alone has failed to solve problems of alcohol abuse and binge drinking. Schools must also institute tougher alcohol policies on campuses, such as moving students with multiple alcohol violations to separate dorms and working to reduce the number of alcohol retailers in near campus. Research indicates that the heavy drinkers are in the minority, and that most students support stronger anti-alcohol measures.

Since results from our first survey were published five years ago [1994], heavy episodic alcohol use or "binge drinking" among college students has become a nationally recognized problem. Seventy percent of college presidents consider binge drinking a problem for their institutions, but they don't know how to counteract it. This is no surprise, since there has not, up to now, been sufficient, scientifically credible information about what is effective. Some approaches seem promising, but they usually have been evaluated on a single campus only, often without control groups.

In this article, we are now able to offer selected findings from our College Alcohol Study (CAS) that can be used to shape intervention campaigns to address the problem of binge drinking. Since 1993, over 50,000 students in a nationally representative sample of 140 colleges in 39 states have responded to our three surveys. We've asked questions about alcohol use and abuse, experience with prevention programs, encounters with enforcement or control policies, and attitudes toward school initiatives. We've learned a number of important lessons to guide college responses to student alcohol abuse.

There is general agreement today about the nature of the problem. The CAS national findings clearly demonstrate that binge drinking is prevalent on most college campuses. Nationally, two in five students binge drink—defined as consuming five or more drinks in a row for men and four for women—at least once in a two-week period. These students experience a higher rate of various educational, social, and health problems than their non-binging peers. Half of the students who binge drink do so more than once a week. Half of these frequent binge drinkers report having five or more different alcohol-related problems during the school year. This rate is 20 times greater than that for students who drink but do not binge.

Beyond the harm they cause for themselves, binge drinkers affect others on campus. Non-binging students who attend schools in which more than half of the students binge drink are more than twice as likely to report such secondhand effects as insults and arguments, vandalism, physical assaults, or unwanted sexual advances than are students in schools with fewer binge drinkers.

Each year, one in eight students reports injuries resulting from alcohol use.

At most campuses, these problems are just too severe to ignore. While deaths are relatively rare, most large colleges report numerous overdoses—admissions for acute alcoholic poisonings—in their student health centers or community emergency rooms. In our survey, 0.6 percent of students report needing treatment for alcohol overdose. While this seems like a small number, projected nationally it could add up to over 30,000 students a year. Each year, one in eight students reports injuries resulting from alcohol use, and one in 20 reports injuries severe enough to require medical treatment.

Binge drinking also affects students' academic performance, with half of binge drinkers reporting that they missed at least one class as a result of their alcohol use, and more than a third saying they fell behind in their schoolwork due to drinking. Binge drinkers are also more likely to report lower grades than non-bingers.

Colleges must protect their students from these negative effects of alcohol. One in eight non-binge-drinking students nationwide reported being assaulted physically or having personal property vandalized due to another student's alcohol use. The everyday effects of binge drinking disrupt the process of higher education. Taking care of drunks, having sleep and study disturbed, and worrying about one's physical safety are incompatible with the atmosphere required for optimal learning to take place.

One size does not fit all

Binge drinking rates at different colleges range from one to 80 percent of students. This variation suggests that institutional approaches should be shaped by the particular conditions of a given campus. Many factors—the attitudes and experiences students bring to school, social and institutional features of the college, and characteristics of the adjoining community—contribute to student alcohol problems. Colleges vary with respect to each of these factors, including for example, the levels of drinking during high school by their incoming freshman, the size and status of their fraternities and sororities, and the number and political strength of local alcohol outlets. The response of colleges must take these variations into account; there are no "one-size-fits-all" solutions. While we here offer national statistics that can be used in shaping campaigns, each college needs to take stock of its own particular situation. A comprehensive self-diagnosis is the necessary first step.

Alcohol education is not enough

A natural response for colleges wishing to address binge drinking is to educate students about the problems of alcohol use. Results from our surveys of college administrators indicate that curriculum infusion, dedicated classes, and poster or communications campaigns are a regular part of most school efforts. Student reports reflect this educational emphasis. Four of five students have been exposed to some alcohol education effort. Two of three students have seen posters or signs and report having read announcements or articles.

The problem, however, is that most of the heaviest drinkers too easily ignore all this; indeed, they do not view their drinking as a problem. Only one-quarter of the frequent binge drinkers say they ever had a drinking problem; two of three students who drink that way consider themselves "moderate drinkers."

While education is needed, by itself it will not solve the problem. Binge drinkers, in fact, are more likely than non-binge drinkers to report they have received information from the school. Moreover, the most at-risk groups on campus—members of Greek organizations and athletes—are already targeted for educational interventions in an over-whelming majority of survey schools. Eighty percent of schools report offering special educational programs for athletes, while two-thirds offer programs for fraternity members and 60 percent for sorority members.

In other words, college students have been told about the risks of alcohol use, yet they continue to binge drink. While our evidence demonstrates that schools are targeting the right audiences for their interventions, it suggests that the impact is limited. Reliance solely on educational interventions to reduce alcohol use is an inadequate response. Colleges need to move beyond a simple didactic model.

Student support for tougher policies

Many colleges are considering an increase in controls over alcohol; pressures to do so have risen in the wake of a number of highly visible deaths on college campuses in the past two years. Administrators are caught between the fear that a tragic event will occur if they don't tighten controls over alcohol and the threat of student protests and potential riots if they do. While our results indicate that colleges that ban alcohol for everyone on campus—including of-age students—have lower rates of binge drinking and associated problems, the causal direction of this relationship is not clear. It may be that it is easier to ban alcohol at colleges with low binge rates, or that a third factor—such as a shared concern among students and administrators over the negative effects of heavy drinking—is responsible for both the lower rates and the strict policy.

While education is needed, by itself it will not solve the problem.

When considering whether to adopt tougher control measures, it should not be a foregone conclusion that students will strongly oppose such a change. Some will, as the still vivid memories of students throwing debris at police or burning furniture in protest suggest. However, our data indicate that many students are concerned about the role alcohol plays in their life at college. Half of all students nationally believe that alcohol is a problem on their campus; considerable support exists for a wide array of possible policy controls. Among colleges that strengthened their alcohol policies between 1993 and 1997, nearly one-quarter did so in response to pressure from students.

Table 1: Student Support for Tougher Measures to Reduce Binge Drinking	
Possible Policy Controls	Percentage Support
Crack down on underage drinking	67
Enforce rules strictly	65
Prohibit kegs on campus	60
Crack down on Greeks	60
Hold hosts responsible	55
Ban ads from local outlets	52

College administrators should realize that they have a lot more support to implement policy changes than they think they do. Although this may come as a surprise to administrators confronted by angry students demanding the "right" to drink as much as they want, more than half of all students nationally favor more college intervention. As Table 1 shows, there is considerable student support for a wide array of possible policy controls that may help impact binge drinking and related harms.

Marginalizing the heaviest drinkers

Frequent binge drinkers are out of touch with the way alcohol problems are perceived by others on campus. Only one in five students engages in this type of drinking, yet this group accounts for two-thirds of all the alcohol consumed by college students; more than half of all the alcohol-related problems students experience; and over 60 percent of all the reported injuries, vandalism, and problems with the police.

While most of these students don't think they have a problem with alcohol, their schools have a problem with them. Frequent binge drinkers oppose efforts by college administrators to reduce levels of problem drinking and related harms. These are the students most likely to protest, not always peacefully, in support of the item most important to them: beer. But in this stance, they are out of step with most other students, even the occasional binge drinkers. A look at support of tougher control measures by type of drinker (Table 2) reveals how out of touch frequent binge drinkers are.

Table 2: National-Level Student Support for Tougher Policies (Percentages)

| | Non- | Drinkers | | |
Policy	Drinkers	Occasional	Frequent	Bingers
Prohibit kegs on campus	86.4	67.7	48.6	34.6
Enforce rules strictly	93.2	75.0	54.2	35.2
Crack down on Greeks	90.1	69.5	47.1	28.2
Hold hosts responsible	81.1	59.9	45.3	33.3
Crack down on underage drinkers	93.5	76.9	56.6	37.1

Administrators and students need to appreciate that the heaviest drinkers are a vocal, highly visible, but relatively small minority. Up to now, given peer pressure to drink, non-bingers have often felt marginalized, with the best they could ask for being separate, alcohol-free dorms. The segregation should work the other way, with students who disturb the peace moved to dorms for people whose behaviors indicate they need extra supervision.

Low-cost alcohol is a high-cost problem

When students are looking for social activities, few alternatives can compete with the low cost of alcohol. A recent survey of bars and retail liquor outlets in 10 college communities makes this point very clearly. (See Table 3.)

Administrators and students need to appreciate the fact that the heaviest drinkers are a vocal, highly visible, but relatively small minority.

Social activities that involve alcohol appeal to students on a cost basis. Alcohol is cheap, plentiful, and easy to get. For the price of one movie ticket (not including concessions), a student could buy eight drinks at a bar, 15 cans of beer, or entrance for three people to an "all-you-can-drink-party." On all of these campuses, students can find a way to binge drink for less than five dollars. Students who pay less than a dollar per drink, or who pay a set fee for "all-you-can-drink," are more likely to drink at binge levels than students who have to pay more. Econometric analyses of alcohol use have shown that price does play a role in binge drinking, particularly among women.

A high density of alcohol outlets surrounds most larger campuses. Establishments cater to college students and compete with each other to draw business. Frequently this competition translates into price wars: local outlets undercut each other and make up the difference by selling large volumes. College communities can examine the distribution of liquor outlets and the pricing practices in the neighborhoods around them. They can then begin a process of dialogue and concerted action with community leaders to solve these problems.

Designated helpers

College students are motivated by positive messages that align with their values. They tend to be less responsive to rule-based approaches than to positive visions of their role. Indeed, social factors—like the number of close friends and hours spent socializing with friends—are important predictors of binge drinking, independent of age, religion, personal and family alcohol history, and other substance use.

Table 3: Cost of Alcohol Compared with Other Student Activities at 10 High-Binge Universities

Social Activities	Average Price
Beer from a keg	$0.25
Beer from a can	$0.37
Drink special at bars/clubs	$0.75
Admission, all-you-can-drink party	$1.50
Cup of coffee (off-campus)	$1.09
Movie ticket	$5.86
Concert	$27.33

One norm among students that can be a very powerful motivator is their desire to see that their friends are safe. Half of students nationally report that they have taken care of another student who was drunk, an important indicator of student values. Positive messages can capitalize on these existing motivations and reinforce safe behaviors.

Anti-drunk-driving campaigns have profited from similar messages promoting informal controls of drinking behavior among friends. This approach may hold even more promise for college students: messages can appeal to their desire to protect their friends. "Friends don't let friends drive drunk" is a message that resonates with a highly social group. Similar messages aimed at students can enhance peer support for discouraging others from getting drunk, acting irresponsibly, having sex when they are drunk, or burdening their friends with unsafe behavior. "Friends don't let friends lose control" may be an appropriate message for students who fear the secondhand effects of alcohol or the increasingly litigious repercussions of going out or hooking up while under the influence.

Another message that can resonate is that in group situations, some students owe it to others to abstain. In some of the recent, highly publicized overdose deaths, the people who were taking care of the student who died were also intoxicated and unable to recognize the seriousness of the situation.

Women are affected at lower dosage levels of alcohol than men. In our survey, we employed a gender-specific measure of binge drinking to account for the greater number of problems women experience at the same consumption rate as men. Women who join sororities have had fewer binge-drinking experiences in high school than men who join fraternities, yet in college they binge drink at the same rate as men. The mix of alcohol and inexperience puts them in grave jeopardy for sexual assault. Acquaintance rape is one of the most salient health issues for women on college campuses. Nationally, one of 10 female frequent binge drinkers reported engaging in non-consensual sex while under the influence of alcohol.

Female students are an important target group for promoting mutual caretaking messages. Informally today we already see women designated to stay sober and watch out for their friends at heavy drinking parties.

Many college campuses have well-established women's centers that are credible and effective advocates for women's health and status. The staff of these centers need to be concerned about the ways in which binge drinking and alcohol abuse are women's health issues. Women's centers on colleges should be partners in efforts to reduce binge drinking and related harms.

Enablers may disable

It is especially important to pay attention to mutual caretaking motives in light of the evidence on how underage students obtain alcohol.

A great deal of collegiate energy and prevention resources are spent on combating fake IDs. Yet this technique for obtaining alcohol is used by only one in five underage students. How do they get alcohol? Four of five underage drinkers get their alcohol from older students. One-third of older students have been asked by underage students to provide them with alcohol, and almost all complied. This is one student norm that needs to be challenged!

Of-age students view providing alcohol to minors as a gesture of friendship and don't consider the potential for harm. To them, this form of sharing is a positive act. We need to make a clear distinction for these students between positive and negative acts of "sharing" alcohol. What kind of "friendship" would enable heavy drinking?

Student rights

While we hear from students demanding a right to drink, there have been few public demonstrations for a binge-free college environment. According to our data, most college students have experienced secondhand effects of binge drinking, but few complain about it. Seven in eight non-binge-drinking students have been affected negatively by the drinking of others, yet only one of seven students living in dormitories reports having complained to a resident advisor about other students' drinking. Students may choose not to complain due to social pressure or fear of retaliation.

The change needed is for all students to understand that they have far more fundamental rights as students than any claimed "right" of a few to drink. The rights of all students to live and learn in a habitable dormitory environment need to be reestablished as a part of college policy addressing binge drinking. A campaign that informs students of their basic right to a quality of campus life free from the secondhand effects of binge drinking is needed. Agreement with student governments about unacceptable behavior in a group living situation, and enforcement of the resulting code of conduct, is an important step toward reducing the harms of excessive alcohol use.

Students almost universally support alcohol-free living environments. Nearly nine out of every 10 students support a policy by colleges that would provide alcohol-free dormitories on campus. Some have voted already with their feet. Eighteen percent of students report that they already live in an alcohol-free dorm; 24 percent more say they would like to live in one. Altogether, three of five non-bingers either live in—or want to live in—an alcohol-free dorm.

Binge drinking is the most serious problem affecting social life, health, and education on college campuses today. Colleges should develop campaigns specifically tailored for their campuses, using our survey data as a start, and using what they know about local problems and resources. On a national level, our overall recommendations point to issues that deserve attention. These issues lend themselves to local campaigns undertaken by college administrators, communications experts, and prevention specialists.

Colleges Should Promote Moderate Drinking

Franklin B. Krohn

Franklin B. Krohn is a professor in the department of business administration at the State University of New York College at Fredonia.

Alcohol abuse on college campuses has been a longstanding problem. However, prohibition of all drinking on campus is an unlikely goal because college students are subjected to strong social pressures to drink. Moderation is a more realistic goal for college students. Moderate drinking has been shown to have health, academic, and behavioral advantages compared to excessive drinking. Ultimately, moderate drinking is the most realistic goal for colleges wanting to combat the problem of alcohol abuse.

Alcohol has increasingly become a determining factor in the scholastic success and retention rates of college students across the nation. The abuses associated with alcohol consumption have also triggered many campus organizations to design alcohol awareness programs, which focus on prohibiting and or completely eliminating the use of alcohol on college campuses. These goals appear to be unrealistic for the modern college student, who is subjected to the social pressures that exist on campuses. These pressures include (1) conformity, (2) compliance, (3) obedience, and (4) social diversity.

Social pressures

First, conformity occurs when individuals change their attitudes or behavior to follow social norms. Often, college students are expected to consume excessive amounts of alcohol, which alter states of action and integration within the group. Conformity to such risky behavior can be increased by cohesiveness and with the number of people pressuring such actions. Most people conform to the social norms of their group most of the time because of two powerful needs possessed by all human beings: the desire to be liked or accepted by others, and the desire to be right. Additionally, cognitive processes lead to viewing conformity as fully justified after it has occurred.

The desire to be liked is explained by normative social influence, which is social influence based on individuals' desire to be liked or accepted by other persons. Most people try to appear to be as similar to others as possible. One reason people conform is that they learn that by doing so they can win the approval and acceptance human beings crave.

Second, compliance involves efforts by one or more individuals to change the behaviors of others. In general, people are more willing to comply with requests from friends or from people liked than requests from strangers or people not liked. This principle is referred to as friendship/liking. Many students comply with excessive drinking patterns because their friends reinforce the behavior. Many fraternities and sororities are guilty of ingratiation: getting others to like them so that they will be more willing to agree to their requests. Increased liking can in turn lead to greater compliance.

Student drinking is the number one health problem on college and university campuses throughout the country.

Third, the most direct form of social influence is obedience. Obedience is yielding to direct orders from another person to do something. Obedience is less frequent than conformity or compliance, but deserves attention in social influences of college students. Research findings indicate that people often obey commands from authority figures or upperclassmen even when such people have little or no authority to enforcing the requests. Individuals can resist obedience through making a positive choice to decline the command.

Fourth, social diversity involving gender differences in social influence appears not significant in susceptibility to social influence among equal status persons. Early studies on this issue seemed to indicate that women are more susceptible than men. Later studies, however, point that there are no significant differences between males and females in this respect. The reversal occurred because the early studies used materials and tasks more familiar to males, which placed females at a disadvantage to conformity pressure. . . .

Controlling the pressure

In order to control and punish, there are a number of approaches: (1) current laws increase liabilities for those who serve alcoholic beverages to minors, (2) hold universities liable for not intervening, (3) charge alcohol establishments for violations of intervention, and (4) have reduced the fraternal experience.

First, contributing parties providing alcohol to underage drinkers are held liable for serving alcohol to minors whether it is a bar establishment or a social gathering among friends. This violation is punishable via fines or jail sentencing. Second, a new strategy of reformists is to hold universities liable in cases in which the college did not intervene to subdue the consumption problems. This liability is often invoked at universities that have fraternities and sororities on campus. Third, Dram Shop Laws establish that saloons are liable for contributing to excessive drunkenness. Bar establishments have also lost liquor licenses for serving alcoholic beverages to minors, those under the legal drinking age of 21. Fourth, the social and economic harm of alcohol abuse threatens the survival of the collegiate Greek system in the United States. Poor scholarship, low rush numbers, poor retention of members, personal injuries and property damages are some of the results of excessive drinking patterns. A popular argument made by students is that alcohol prohibition on college campuses hinders the social experience. Many students view these radical changes as an infringement of their social life.

Alcohol facts

Compulsive drinking in excess has become one of modern society's most serious problems. Many people do not view alcohol as a drug, largely because its uses for religious and social purposes are common, however, the effects depend on the amount consumed at a specific time.

Table 1: Amount of Alcohol in the Blood and the Effects	
(mg/dL)	EFFECT
	Mild Intoxication
	Feeling of warmth, skin flushed; impaired judgment; decreased inhibitions
100	Obvious Intoxication In Most People
	Increased impairment of judgment, inhibition, attention, and control; some impairment of muscular performance; slowing of reflexes
150	Obvious Intoxication In All Normal People
	Staggering gait and other muscular incoordination; slurred speech; double vision; memory and comprehension loss
250	Extreme Intoxication or Stupor
	Reduced response to stimuli; inability to stand; vomiting; incontinence; sleepiness
350	Coma
	Unconsciousness; little response to stimuli; incontinence; low body temperature; poor respiration; fall in blood pressure; clammy skin
500	Death Likely
Addiction Research Foundation	

Once alcohol enters the body it is rapidly absorbed into the bloodstream from the small intestine. Alcohol contamination in the blood leads to slower activity in parts of the brain as well as the spinal cord. The drinker's blood alcohol concentration depends on the amount consumed, the drinker's sex, size, and metabolism, and the type and amount of food in the stomach. The effects of alcohol depend on the amount consumed at one time (see Table 1).

Harmful consequences of alcohol consumption vary from person to person, however, the effects remain similar. Drinking heavily over a short period will result in a "hangover," due to poisoning by alcohol and the body's reaction to withdrawal from alcohol. Combining alcohol with other drugs can make the effects of these other drugs much stronger and more dangerous. Some of these harmful consequences are primary, resulting directly from prolonged exposure to alcohol's toxic effects such as liver disease. Other consequences are secondary. They are indirectly related to chronic alcohol abuse, such as loss of appetite, vitamin deficiencies, and sexual impotence.

Alcohol and the student

Student drinking is the number one health problem on college and university campuses throughout the country. College students are at a higher risk for alcohol related problems because they have high rates of heavy consumption (binge drinking), tend to drink more recklessly than others, and are heavily targeted by advertising and promotions of the alcoholic beverage industry. Students spend approximately $4.2 billion annually to purchase 430 million gallons of alcoholic beverages. Alcohol is associated with missed classes and poor performance on tests and projects. The number of alcoholic drinks consumed per week is clearly related to lower GPAs.

Campuses throughout the nation have been assisted in combating this pressing problem by the U.S. Drug-Free Schools and Communities Act Amendments of 1989. It requires that institutions of higher learning receiving Federal funds attest that they have adopted and implemented a drug prevention program for both students and employees. One example offered to students is peer counseling. Many colleges train peer counselors to educate groups and individuals about the dangers of alcohol use. Some colleges limit or ban alcohol advertising in student newspapers and sponsorship of student events by alcoholic beverage companies. Another solution offered to students is alcohol-free residence halls. An emerging trend is for colleges to establish residence halls where students sign pledges that they will not use alcohol, tobacco, or other drugs. How effective this strategy is has yet to be determined.

Nevertheless, social acceptance of this drug still remains. These laws have neither crippled nor eliminated the problem. The more a behavior is suppressed, often the more it occurs. The alcoholic prohibition experiment in the United States was very revealing about American culture.

Prohibition

Attempts to prohibit alcohol usage have been made since colonial times. Temperance movements began to gain sizable support by the public and government. The first national temperance society was formed in 1836. The temperance movement led to the adoption of full prohibition, rather than just temperance alone. Since the major parties of the political sphere refused to take a stance on the prohibition issue, a third party known as the Prohibition Party was formed in 1869. Although the party was never successful, their ideas spread throughout the country.

The prohibition movement reached its peak in the late 19th century, however, it was not until the southwestern states turned to prohibition that the issue gained mass popularity. There were many factors leading to the passage of this ineffective legislation. In order to conserve grain during World War I, federal legislation passed a series of laws to help ration supplies that were needed for the effort. This rationing established the roots for prohibition legislation. The national prohibition amendment was ratified by all but two states on January 16, 1919 and went into effect one year later. Between 1920 and 1933 prohibition was in effect in the United States. Prohibition is the illegality of manufacturing, selling, or transporting any type of alcoholic beverage.

The more a behavior is suppressed, often the more it occurs.

Even though the prohibition amendment was passed by an overwhelming majority in Congress, it soon became evident that the amendment was unenforceable. The enforcement was minimized because the 1920s saw a revolution in social (1) manners, (2) customs, and (3) habits, which led to mass inclination to ignore existing prohibition legislation. "Prohibition did not achieve its goals. Instead, it added to the problems it was intended to solve." Prohibition caused an explosive growth in crime and increased the amount of alcohol consumption. There were also numerous speak-easies which replaced saloons after the start of prohibition. Approximately only five percent of smuggled liquor was hindered from coming into the country in the 1920s. Furthermore, the illegal liquor business fell under the control of organized gangs, which overpowered most of the law enforcement authorities. As a result of the lack of enforcement of the Prohibition Act and the creation of an illegal industry, an overall increase in crime transpired. The problems prohibition intended to solve, such as crime, grew worse and they never returned to their pre-prohibition levels.

The major goal of the 18th Amendment was to abolish the saloon. By outlawing the manufacturing and sale of alcohol only, the patronage of a bootlegger emerged. The Volstead Act was intended to prohibit intoxicating beverages, regulate the manufacture, production and use of spirits other than beverage purposes, and promote scientific research in the development of lawful purposes. Initially, all of these regulations were left for the Treasury Department to oversee. The ineffectiveness in preventing illegal diversions and arresting bootleggers led to the creation of the Prohibition Bureau. This was another incompetent strategy based on the spoils system which filled positions with men who discredited the enforcement efforts.

Prohibition was intended to solve over-consumption of alcohol, but inevitably encouraged consumption. A clause in the Volstead Act made search and seizure virtually unobtainable because any warrant issued was dependent on proof that the liquor was for sale. No matter how much alcohol a person had at home, and no matter how it was obtained or used, agents of the bureau had to have positive evidence that a commercial transaction took place. This requirement inadvertently promoted home and cottage industry manufacturing of liquor. For example, during the first five years of Prohibition, the acreage of vineyards increased 700 percent, accompanied by insincere warning labeling such as "do not place liquid in bottle away in the cupboard for twenty days, because it would turn into wine." Although possession of illegally obtained alcohol was prohibited, the act of drinking alcohol was legal. This suggests that even prohibitionists understood the limits of regulating individual behavior.

Data on alcohol prohibition on campuses across the nation have also had little success in solving or finding a solution to this unrelenting problem. One purpose of this paper is to explore whether there is another approach that might be taken to better equip the college student in becoming a responsible alcohol consumer.

Moderation

All societies in which alcohol is consumed employ a range of strategies to minimize the harm associated with its use. The most effective public policies are those that affect the environment of drinking or influence the drinker's demand for alcohol. These include taxation and price policies, controls on access to alcohol such as limiting the condition and time of sale, modifying the drinking environment, a minimum legal drinking age, and countermeasures against drinking in hazardous circumstances such as when driving.

A moderate drinker is defined as one who imbibes one five-ounce glass of wine, one 12-ounce beer, or 1 1/2 shots of liquor daily. Consuming alcohol above these amounts can be hazardous. However, moderating the amount of alcohol intake can be beneficial. These benefits include (1) health, (2) scholastic performance, and (3) a decline in violence.

Prohibition was intended to solve over-consumption of alcohol, but inevitably encouraged consumption.

First, heavy consumption of alcoholic beverages is linked to many health problems. Excessive use impairs the body's nervous system resulting in a lack of fine motor skills, reaction speed, and visual perception. Alcohol also causes one to tire faster because it weakens the heart's pumping force. The human body recognizes the alcohol as a toxin and metabolizes it before anything else. Thus, the body cannot burn more fuel efficient fats and proteins. In addition, too much alcohol may cause cirrhosis of the liver, inflammation of the pancreas, damage to the brain and heart, and increased risks for some cancers. Limiting intake of alcohol makes room for foods that provide important nutrients. For all these reasons, drinking alcoholic beverages excessively is not recommended. If students choose to drink them, they should drink them only in moderate amounts or drink alternatives. Alternatives to alcoholic beverages include a mixer or fruit juice, complete with a garnish but without the alcohol.

There have been numerous studies which support the health benefits of moderate drinking. Moderate drinkers tend to have better health and live longer than those who are either abstainers or heavy drinkers. In addition to having fewer heart attacks and strokes, moderate consumers of alcohol are generally less likely to suffer hypertension or high blood pressure, peripheral artery disease, Alzheimer's disease and the common cold.

Second, students who consume alcoholic beverages moderately achieve higher scholastic achievement than excessive consumers of alcohol beverages. Alcohol abuse is associated with poor academic performance. According to a national research, 21 percent of binge drinkers fell behind in their studies and 30 percent missed class during the school year.

Third, excessive alcohol consumption contributes to violence in multiple ways, chiefly by increasing aggression, particularly when the blood alcohol level rises rapidly (such as with binge drinking). Several studies estimate that between 50 percent and 80 percent of violence on campus is alcohol related. In addition, many students believe intoxication excuses inappropriate and violent behavior. A study of women who were victims of some type of sexual aggression while in college, from rape to intimidation and illegal restraint, found that 68 percent of their male assailants had been drinking at the time of the attack.

Having control over the amount of alcohol consumption allows people to make better judgments for safety and health purposes. Social drinkers use alcohol in moderate amounts, while alcoholics do not limit their intake. The first step to moderation is practicing safe use of the drug. This means setting boundaries for the amount of alcohol consumed. After establishing a salubrious program, maintenance is the key to continuous moderate use of alcoholic beverages.

Colleges should moderate

There is no simple solution to the alcohol abuse that occurs at colleges and universities across the nation. After examining two opposite methods to control alcohol abuse across college campuses, moderation is a conceivable and attainable goal. Campus administrators should promote moderation as opposed to forbidding the use of alcohol at universities. The acknowledgement of excessive alcohol abuse on campuses is only the first step. Offering alternatives to students, such as moderation lead to solving the problem. It is inconceivable to believe that no calamitous events will occur with both widespread acceptance of alcohol and the heavy promotion by alcohol manufacturers; however, taking the moderation approach is more feasible than outright prohibition.

9

Drug Therapy Is an Effective Treatment for Alcohol Abuse

Donald W. Goodwin

Donald W. Goodwin was a professor of psychiatry at the University of Kansas and the author of several books on alcoholism, including Is Alcoholism Hereditary? *and* Alcoholism: The Facts, *from which this viewpoint is excerpted.*

Antabuse, a drug that makes people physically ill when they drink, has been the most widely used drug for alcohol therapy for the past 25 years. Antabuse has had a controversial history due to early deaths cause by overdoses of the drug. However, Antabuse promises a recovery from alcoholism as long as the patient complies with the doctor's orders to take Antabuse and to see the doctor every 3 to 5 days, so that the doctor can facilitate the recovery process by identifying any underlying emotional or psychological problem that may be contributing to the patient's problems with alcohol. Critics have charged that treatment with Antabuse essentially instills a fear of drinking in the patient, but a fear-based cure for alcoholism is justifiable if it results in success.

In Sears Roebuck mail order catalogues at the turn of the century two pages were devoted to drug therapies for morphine addiction and alcoholism, respectively. The drug being sold for morphine addiction consisted mainly of alcohol; a good part of the drug for alcoholism consisted of tincture of opium, a relative of morphine. Whether morphine addicts became alcoholics as a result of the treatment, or vice versa, is not known, but it illustrates the long history of giving one drug that affects mood and behaviour to relieve the effects of another drug that affects mood and behaviour. Substitution therapy reached a pinnacle with the widespread, officially sanctioned, and probably useful substitution of methadone (an addicting substance like heroin) for heroin. Heroin itself was introduced at the turn of the century as a 'heroic' cure for morphine addiction and was also believed to be useful for alcoholism. It has not done much for either condition, although a drug that blocks the effects of heroin called Naltrexone has been reported recently to promote abstinence from alcohol.

The dubious history of using drugs to cure addiction

Drugs are still widely prescribed to alcoholics. They mainly consist of drugs for anxiety, such as Ativan and Valium, and drugs for depression. The anti-anxiety drugs have some effects similar to those of alcohol—they calm and relax—and are useful in relieving the jitteriness that follows heavy drinking, so that they may be useful in stopping a drinking bout. Whether they stop the *resumption* of drinking—the test of a drug's true worth in treating alcoholism—is debatable, and many clinicians feel they do not.

These drugs are sometimes used in excess by alcoholics, and sometimes in combination with alcohol. This may not be as harmful as it sounds since they have a low range of toxicity and few people become addicted in the literal sense of needing increasingly larger amounts and having serious withdrawal symptoms when they stop taking them. Nevertheless, they have obviously contributed little to the management of alcoholism, and some clinicians feel strongly that they should not be given to alcoholics for extended periods.

With one exception, there is no evidence that antidepressant medications are useful in the treatment of alcoholism, although some alcoholics do become seriously depressed and antidepressant drugs may then be indicated for their depression. The exception is a group of drugs that enhance the neurotransmitter serotonin in its effect on brain cells. Prozac is a member of this group. These drugs reduce drinking in animals *and* humans. . . . Lithium, a drug useful in the treatment of mania, has been given to alcoholics, and early reports indicated that some people benefited from it. Since early reports often indicate that a particular treatment is useful, only to be refuted by later reports, lithium therapy was viewed with both interest and scepticism. The scepticism was reinforced when a large multi-hospital study in the USA failed to find the lithium was useful for alcoholism. One clinical observation that lends support to the possibility that lithium *might* be useful is that people with manic-depressive disease often drink more when they are manic than when they are depressed.

From a theoretical viewpoint, it is interesting that anti-anxiety and most antidepressant drugs do not seem to deter alcoholics from using alcohol. There is ample evidence that these drugs do indeed relieve anxiety and depression, and if alcoholics drink because they feel anxious and depressed, one would assume that the drugs would substitute for alcohol more than they seem to do. . . .

Other treatments that have been tried are LSD and large doses of vitamins, with no convincing evidence they help.

Antabuse is different

Perhaps the drug most commonly prescribed for alcoholism over the past 25 years is one that has no effect on anxiety or depression or apparently anything else *unless* combined with alcohol. This, of course, is Antabuse.

The drug makes people physically ill when they drink. When it was first used in the early fifties, Antabuse got a bad name for two reasons. First, like most highly touted treatments, it was not the panacea its enthusiastic supporters had hoped it would be. Second, some people taking the drug died after drinking. It was later learned that the drug could be given in smaller amounts and still produce an unpleasant reaction when combined with alcohol, but death was exceedingly rare.

Partly because of the bad reputation it obtained in the early years, it has perhaps been underused since then. The more dogmatic members of AA view Antabuse as somehow incompatible with the spirit of AA, and many alcoholics resist taking the drug on the grounds that it is a 'crutch.'

[There is a] long history of giving one drug that affects mood and behaviour to relieve the effects of another drug that affects mood and behaviour.

Antabuse has not been entirely popular with doctors for another reason. Some still believe they must give an Antabuse 'challenge' test before prescribing the drug for indefinite periods. This test consists of giving the patient Antabuse for a few days and then giving him a small amount of alcohol to demonstrate what an Antabuse reaction is like. The Antabuse challenge test is no longer considered necessary or even desirable. Patients can be told what the effects of Antabuse will be and this will have the same effect. One awkward aspect of the challenge test is that some patients have no reaction when given the alcohol, simply because people react very differently to both alcohol and Antabuse and the cautious doses of alcohol administered are too small to produce an effect.

The main problem with Antabuse, however, is not that patients drink after taking the drug but that they stop taking the drug because they 'forget' to take it or convince themselves the drug is causing side-effects, such as impotency. . . .

Something that works, provided . . .

There is an approach to treating alcoholism that works every time, given one stipulation: the patient must do what the doctor says. In this case he must do only one thing: come to the office every three or four days.

Doctors cannot help patients, as a rule, who refuse to do what they say, so there is nothing unusual about the stipulation. Why every three or four days? Because the effects of Antabuse last up to five days after a person takes it. If the patient takes Antabuse in the office, in the presence of the doctors, they both *know* he will not drink for up to five days. They have bought time, a precious thing in the treatment of alcoholism.

This approach involves other things besides Antabuse, but Antabuse makes the other things possible. First it gives hope, and hope by the time the alcoholic sees a doctor is often in short supply. He feels his case is hopeless, his family feels it is hopeless, and often the doctor feels it is hopeless. With this approach the doctor can say, 'I can help you with your drinking problem' and mean it. He doesn't mean he can help him forever (forever is a long time) and it doesn't mean the patient won't still be unhappy or that he will become a new man. It merely means he will not drink as long as he comes to the office every three or four days and takes the Antabuse. Properly warned, he won't drink unless he is crazy or stupid, and if either is the case, he probably should not be given Antabuse. On the first visit the doctor can say something like this:

> Your problem, or at least your immediate problem, is that you have trouble controlling your drinking. Let *me* take charge; let me control your drinking for a time. This will be my responsibility. Come in, take the pill, and then we can deal with other things.

> I want you to stop drinking for a month. [At this point the doctor makes a note in his desk calendar to remind himself when the patient will have taken Antabuse for a month.] After that we can discuss whether you want to continue taking the pill. It will be your decision.

> You need to stop for a month for two reasons. First, I need to know whether there is anything wrong with you besides drinking too much. You may have another problem that I can treat, such as a depression, but I won't be able to find out until you stop drinking for at least several weeks. Alcohol itself makes people depressed and anxious, and mimics all kinds of psychiatric illnesses.

> Second, I want you to stop drinking for a month to have a chance to see that life is bearable—sometimes just barely bearable—without alcohol. Millions of people don't drink and manage. You can manage too, but you haven't had a chance recently to discover this.

F. Scott Fitzgerald complained that he could never get sober long enough to tolerate sobriety, and at least this much can be achieved with the present approach.

It is important for the patient to see the doctor (or whatever professional is responsible for his care) whenever he comes for the pill. Patients as a rule want to please their doctors; this is probably why they are more punctual in keeping office appointments than doctors are in seeing them. In the beginning the patient may be coming, in part, as a kind of favour to the doctor.

The visits can be as brief or as long as time permits. The essential thing is that rapport be established, that the patient believe something is being done to help him, and that he stay on the wagon (he has no choice if he lives up to his part of the doctor-patient contract). Brief, frequent visits can accomplish these things.

Helping the patient deal with sobriety

The emphasis during the visit should be not on the pill but on the problems most alcoholics face when they stop drinking. The major problem is finding out what to do with all the time that has suddenly become available now that drinking can no longer fill it. Boredom is the curse of the non-drinking drinking man. For years, most of the pleasurable things in his life have been associated with drinking: food, sex, companionship, fishing, Sunday-afternoon football. Without alcohol these things lose some of their attraction. The alcoholic tends to withdraw, brood, feel sorry for himself.

The therapist may help him find substitute pleasures—hobbies, social activities not revolving around alcohol, anything that kills time and may give some satisfaction, if not anything as satisfying as a boozy glow. In time he may find these things for himself, but meanwhile life can be awfully monotonous.

[Antabuse] has no effect on anxiety or depression or apparently anything else unless *combined with alcohol.*

Also the patient can bring up problems of living that tend to accumulate when a person has drunk a lot. People usually feel better when they talk about problems, particularly when the listener is warm and friendly and doesn't butt into the conversation by talking about his own problems. The therapist can help by listening even if he cannot solve the problems.

If he is a psychiatrist, he can also do a thorough psychiatric examination, looking for something other than drinking to diagnose and treat. Occasionally (not often) alcoholics turn out to have a depressive illness, phobias, or other psychiatric condition.

One thing the therapist can do is help the patient accept his alcoholism. This is sometimes difficult. Alcoholics have spent most of their drinking careers persuading themselves and others that they do not have a drinking problem. The habit of self-deception, set and hardened over so many years, is hard to break. William James describes this habit with his usual verve and concludes that the alcoholic's salvation begins with breaking it:

> How many excuses does the drunkard find when each new temptation comes! Others are drinking and it would be churlishness to refuse; or it is but to enable him to sleep, or just to get through this job of work; or it isn't drinking, it is because he feels so cold; or it is Christmas Day; or it is a means of stimulating him to make a more powerful resolution in favour of abstinence than any he has hitherto made; or it is just this once, and once doesn't count . . . it is, in fact, anything you like except *being a drunkard.* But if . . . through thick and thin he holds to it that he is a drunkard and nothing else, he is not likely to remain one long. The effort by which he succeeds in keeping the right *name* unwaveringly present to his mind proves to be his saving moral act.

After a month of taking the pill and talking about problems, what happens then? The patient and doctor renegotiate. Almost invariably, in my experience, the patient decides to take the pill for another month. The doctor says okay, and this is the first step in a process that must occur if the patient is going to recover: acceptance of personal responsibility for control of his drinking.

Proceeding on a month-to-month basis is a variation on the AA principle that an alcoholic should take each day as it comes.

For years, alcohol has been the most important thing in the alcoholic's life, or close to it. To be told he can never drink again is about as depressing as anything he can hear. It may not even be true. Studies indicate that a small percentage of alcoholics return to 'normal' drinking for long periods. They tend to be on the low end of the continuum of severity, but not always. 'Controlled' drinking is probably a better term than 'normal' drinking, since alcoholics continue to invest alcohol with a significance that would never occur to the truly normal drinker.

Many people, especially some AA members, reject the notion that alcoholics can ever drink normally. If alcoholism is defined as a permanent inability to drink normally, then obviously any person able to drink normally for a long period was never an alcoholic in the first place. The issue is really one of definition, and those few alcoholics who reported sustained periods of controlled drinking in the studies were at any rate considered alcoholic when they *weren't* drinking normally. Most clinicians would agree that it is a mistake to encourage a severe classical alcoholic to believe he can ever again drink normally, but on the other hand telling him he can never drink again seems unnecessary and may not be true in every case.

When does treatment end? The minimum period is one month because that is the basis for the doctor-patient contract agreed upon in advance. Ideally, however, the treatment should continue for a minimum of six months, with the patient himself making the decision to continue taking Antabuse on a month-to-month basis. Why six months? Because there is evidence that most alcoholics who begin drinking again do so within the first six months following abstention.

A general rule applies here: the longer a patient goes without drinking at all, the shorter the relapse if a relapse occurs. It takes tithe to adapt to a sober way of life. Both the doctor and patient should be prepared for relapses. Alcoholism, by definition, is a chronic relapsing condition, although relapses are not inevitable. It resembles manic-depressive disease in this regard and also has similarities to such chronic medical illnesses as diabetes and multiple sclerosis. When the alcoholic has a relapse, his physician often feels resentful. When his diabetic patient has a relapse because he failed to take insulin, the doctor tends to be more understanding. The reason for this inconsistency is not clear.

Objections to Antabuse treatment

Three objections have been raised concerning the above approach to treating alcoholism. The treatment is said to be based on fear, namely, the fear of getting sick, and fear is held to be one of the least desirable forms of motivation. This is debatable. Fear may be the *only* reason some alcoholics stop drinking. There is evidence that internists have somewhat better success in treating alcoholics than psychiatrists do, and the reason may be that they are in a better position to frighten the patient. They have merely to examine his liver and tell him he may be dead in a year if he keeps on drinking. Innumerable alcoholics have stopped drinking because they were told something like this. Others have stopped because they were afraid of losing their wives or jobs. It is probably no coincidence that the hardest alcoholics to treat are those who have little to lose, those who have already lost their wives, jobs, and health. They have no hope of regaining these. All they have left to lose is their life, and, by now, living has little appeal. Probably the most effective alcoholism-treatment programmes are run by industries, where the patient is an employee and his job depends on staying sober. . . .

The second objection to the approach outlined here is that the patient becomes too dependent on a personal relationship with an authority figure, the physician, which must end at some point. In the treatment of alcoholism, the goal is not so much a lifetime cure (although sometimes this happens) as it is to bring about improvement. If the patient stays sober for longer periods after treatment than he did before, the treatment has been at least a limited success. The physician in any case should discourage a dependent relationship. He can insist upon the patient taking the pill and staying dry for a month (realizing that a month is an arbitrary unit of time and any fixed interval will do), but after that the patient has to realize that he himself has the ultimate responsibility for the control of his drinking.

With [the Antabuse] approach the doctor can say, 'I can help you with your drinking problem' and mean it.

The issue of dependence on authority is particularly relevant for the UK where there is evidence that *supervised Antabuse* is an effective treatment, especially when the supervisor is someone close to a patient, such as a spouse or friend. Turning over supervision to a person who actually lives with the patient is a big advantage. It reduces the number of office visits and also can be carried on for much longer than six months. Sometimes a 'contract' is signed by the therapist, patient, and supervisor. The supervisor may actually watch the patient take the Antabuse, but this is not usually necessary. If the patient starts drinking again, obviously he has not been taking the pill. Standing over an adult and watch him take a pill may have an infantalizing effect on the patient and cause resentment—sometimes sufficient resentment to excuse more drinking. One useful clause in the contract (whether written or verbal) is that the wife promises never to mention her husband's previous drinking in any context as long as he continues taking the Antabuse. The victims in the family—wife, husband, children—remember all the bad things that happen when the drinking member of the family was drunk. It tends to leave a lasting scar on the relationship. Many alcoholics are willing to take Antabuse or do practically anything to stop the nagging and harping about past mis-behaviour.

Supervised Antabuse is a much neglected treatment modality in other countries than the UK. It should be tried elsewhere. It often seems to work. Now, back to my 'American plan' of office supervision.

Finally, the complaint is heard that this approach does not get at the root of the problem; it does not explain how the patient became an alcoholic. This is true but, in my opinion, no one can explain how a person becomes an alcoholic because no one knows the cause of alcoholism. Doctors sometimes blame the patient's upbringing and patients often blame everyday stresses. There is no way to validate either explanation. There is probably no harm in telling the patient that his condition remains a medical mystery. . . .

Excellent treatment

However, if it is ever shown conclusively that some form of alcoholism is influenced by heredity, this would not make the prognosis less favourable or the treatment less helpful. Sometimes, when evidence for a genetic factor is presented, you hear the following: 'But if it is genetic, then you can't do anything about it.' It should be noted that adult onset diabetes is almost certainly a genetic disorder and there are excellent treatments for diabetes.

Organizations to Contact

The editors have compiled the following list of organizations concerned with the issues debated in this book. The descriptions are derived from materials provided by the organizations. All have publications or information available for interested readers. The list was compiled on the date of publication of the present volume; the information provided here may change. Be aware that many organizations take several weeks or longer to respond to inquiries, so allow as much time as possible.

Against Drunk Driving (ADD)
PO Box 397, Station A, Brampton, OH L6V 2L3 Canada
(905) 793-4233 • fax: (905) 793-7035
e-mail: add@netcom.ca • website: www.add.ca

Founded in 1983, ADD is a grassroots organization that strives to reduce death and injury caused by impaired drivers through educating the public about the dangers of drunk driving. ADD's group for young adults, Teen-ADD, holds conferences, workshops, and presentations to raise awareness about the problem of teen drunk driving. ADD publishes the quarterly newsletter *ADDvisor,* selected issues of which are also available on its website.

Al-Anon Family Groups Headquarters
1600 Corporate Landing Parkway, Virginia Beach, VA 23454-5617
(757) 563-1600 • fax: (757) 563-1655
e-mail: WSO@alanon.org • website: www.al-anon.alateen.org

Al-Anon is a fellowship of men, women, and children whose lives have been affected by an alcoholic family member or friend. Alateen consists primarily of teenaged Al-Anon members who hold meetings in order to share experiences and learn how to deal with the effects of another person's drinking. Al-Anon/Alateen publications include several books, the monthly magazine *The Forum,* the semiannual *Al-Anon Speaks Out,* the bimonthly *Alateen Talk,* and pamphlets, such as *To the Mother and Father of an Alcoholic, Dear Mom & Dad,* and *Alcoholism, the Family Disease.*

Alcoholics Anonymous (AA)
Grand Central Station, PO Box 459, New York, NY 10163
(212) 870-3400 • fax: (212) 870-3003
website: www.aa.org

Alcoholics Anonymous is a worldwide fellowship of sober alcoholics, whose recovery is based on Twelve Steps. AA requires no dues or fees and accepts no outside funds. It is self-supporting through voluntary contributions of members. It is not affiliated with any other organization. AA's primary purpose is to carry the AA message to the alcoholic who still suffers. Its publications include the pamphlets *A Brief Guide to Alcoholics Anonymous* and *Young People and AA.*

American Beverage Institute (ABI)
1775 Pennsylvania Ave. NW, Suite 1200, Washington, DC 20006
(202) 463-7110 • fax: (202) 463-7107
e-mail: abi@abionline.org • website: www.abionline.org

The American Beverage Institute is a coalition of restaurants and on-premise retailers committed to the responsible serving of alcoholic beverages. The ABI is involved in research, consumer education, and legislative outreach. It publishes the monthly *ABI Newsletter* and legislative alerts.

Canadian Centre on Substance Abuse (CCSA)
75 Albert St., Suite 300, Ottawa ON K1P 5E7 Canada
(613) 235-4048 ext. 222 • fax: (613) 235-8108
e-mail: info@ccsa.ca • website: www.ccsa.ca

The CCSA is a Canadian clearinghouse on substance abuse. It works to disseminate information on the nature, extent, and consequences of substance abuse and to support and assist organizations involved in substance abuse treatment, prevention, and educational programming. The CCSA publishes reports, policy documents, brochures, research papers, the newsletter *Action News*, and several books, including *Canadian Profile: Alcohol, Tobacco, and Other Drugs.*

Center for Science in the Public Interest (CSPI)—Alcohol Policies Project
1875 Connecticut Ave. NW, Suite 300, Washington, DC 20009
(202) 332-9110 • fax: (202) 265-4954
e-mail: cspi@cspinet.org • website: www.cspinet.org/booze

CSPI launched the Alcohol Policies Project to reduce the devastating health and social consequences of drinking. The project's prevention-oriented policy strategy is aimed at curbing alcohol-related problems by advocating advertising reforms, increased excise taxes, and expanded warning requirements. Its publications include the quarterly newsletter *BoozeNews*, fact sheets on topics such as binge drinking and alcohol advertising, and the report *Last Call for High-Risk Bar Promotions That Target College Students.*

Distilled Spirits Council of the United States (DISCUS)
1250 Eye St. NW, Suite 400, Washington, DC 20005
(202) 628-3544 • fax: (202) 682-8888
website: www.discus.org

The Distilled Spirits Council of the United States is the national trade association representing producers and marketers of distilled spirits sold in the United States. It seeks to ensure the responsible advertising and marketing of distilled spirits to adult consumers. DISCUS fact sheets and pamphlets, including *Social Responsibility and Public Education*, are available at its website.

Hazelden Institute
PO Box 176, 15251 Pleasant Valley Rd., Center City, MN 55012-9640
(800) 329-9000 • fax: (651) 213-4590
e-mail: info@hazelden.org • website: www.hazelden.org

Hazelden is a nonprofit organization dedicated to helping people recover from alcoholism and other addictions. It provides residential and outpatient treatment for adults and young people, programs for families affected by chemical dependency, and training for a variety of professionals. The institute publishes the quarterly newsletter *Hazelden Voice*, the bimonthly newspaper column *Alive & Free*, books, press releases, research reports, and public policy papers.

Moderation Management (MM)
22 West 27th Street, Fifth Floor, New York, NY 10001
(212) 213-6140 ext. 30 • fax: (212) 213-6582
website: www.moderation.org

Moderation Management is a recovery program and national support network for people who have made the decision to reduce their drinking and make other positive lifestyle changes. MM empowers individuals to accept personal responsibility for choosing and maintaining their own recovery path, whether through moderation or abstinence. They offer the book *Moderate Drinking: The Moderation Management Guide for People Who Want to Reduce Their Drinking*, as well as additional suggested reading material, books, pamphlets, and guidelines regarding drinking in moderation.

Mothers Against Drunk Driving (MADD)
511 E. John Carpenter Frwy., #700, Irving, TX 75062
(800) 438-6233
e-mail: info@madd.org • website: www.madd.org

Mothers Against Drunk Driving seeks to act as the voice of victims of drunk-driving accidents by speaking on their behalf to communities, businesses, and educational groups and by providing materials for use in medical facilities and health and driver education programs. Its website's "Under 21" section provides information for teens about alcohol and drunk driving. MADD publishes brochures, the newsletter *MADD in Action*, and *Driven* magazine.

National Association for Children of Alcoholics (NACoA)
11426 Rockville Pike, Suite 100, Rockville, MD 20852
(888) 554-COAS (554-2627) • fax: (301) 468-0987
e-mail: nacoa@erols.com • website: www.health.org/nacoa

NACoA is the only national nonprofit membership organization working on behalf of children of alcoholics. Its mission is to advocate for all children and families affected by alcoholism and other drug dependencies. The association publishes books, pamphlets, videos, educational kits, and the bimonthly *NACoA Network Newsletter*.

National Center on Addiction and Substance Abuse (CASA)
Columbia University, 152 West 57th St., New York, NY 10019
(212) 841-5200 • fax: (212) 956-8020
website: www.casacolumbia.org

The National Center on Addiction and Substance Abuse brings together all professional disciplines needed to study and combat substance abuse, including alcohol abuse. CASA assesses what works in prevention, treatment, and law enforcement; informs Americans about the economic and social costs of substance abuse; and removes the stigma of substance abuse. Publications include the report *Substance Abuse and the American Adolescent: A Report by the Commission on Substance Abuse Among America's Adolescents.*

The National Clearinghouse for Alcohol and Drug Information (NCADI)
PO Box 2345, Rockville, MD 20847-2345
(800) 729-6686 • fax: (301) 468-6433
e-mail: info@health.org • website: www.health.org

The NCADI is the information service of the Center for Substance Abuse Prevention of the Substance Abuse and Mental Health Services Administration in the U.S. Department of Health and Human Services. NCADI is the world's largest resource for current information and materials concerning substance abuse. The organization distributes fact sheets, brochures, pamphlets, monographs, posters, and video tapes and provides prevention, intervention, and treatment resources to families, schools, and professionals. Its publications include *Detoxification from Alcohol and Other Drugs* and *Naltrexone and Alcoholism Treatment.*

National Council on Alcoholism and Drug Dependence (NCADD)
12 West 21st St., New York, NY 10010
(212) 206-6770 • fax: (212) 645-1690
e-mail: national@ncadd.org • website: www.ncadd.org

NCADD is a volunteer health organization that helps individuals overcome addictions, develops substance abuse prevention and education programs for youth, and advises the federal government on drug and alcohol policies. It operates the Campaign to Prevent Kids from Drinking. Publications include fact sheets such as "Alcoholism and Alcohol-Related Problems," brochures, the quarterly newsletter *NCADD Amethyst*, and the monthly newsletter *NCADD Washington Report.*

National Institute on Alcohol Abuse and Alcoholism
Willco Building, 6000 Executive Blvd., Bethesda, MD 20892-7003
(301) 496-4000
e-mail: niaaaweb-r@exchange.nih.gov • website: www.niaaa.nih.gov

NIAAA supports and conducts biomedical and behavioral research on the causes, consequences, treatment, and prevention of alcoholism and alcohol-related problems. Its College Drinking Initiative seeks to provide the NIAAA, policy makers, and college presidents with research on campus prevention and treatment programs. The NIAAA publishes the quarterly journal *Alcohol Research & Health* (formerly *Alcohol Health & Research World*), *Alcohol Alert* bulletins, pamphlets, and reports.

Students Against Destructive Decisions! (SADD)
SADD National, Box 800, Marlboro, MA 01752
(800) 787-5777 • fax: (508) 481-5759
website: www.saddonline.com

Also known as Students Against Driving Drunk, SADD's mission is to prevent underage drinking and drug use and to focus attention on the consequences of other decisions such as smoking, violence, and sexually transmitted diseases. SADD promotes a no-use message of alcohol and other drugs and encourages students not to participate in activities with destructive consequences. It publishes a newsletter, press releases, and also provides a "Contract for Life" that can be used to increase parent-child communication about alcohol and drug-related decisions.

The Wine Institute
425 Market St., Suite 1000, San Francisco, CA 94105
(415) 512-0151 • fax: (415) 442-0742
e-mail: communications@wineinstitute.org
website: www.wineinstitute.org

The Wine Institute introduces and advocates public policy measures to enhance the environment for the responsible consumption and enjoyment of wine. It publishes the monthly newsletter *Newsflash* and the reports "American Health Association Advisory Acknowledges 'Potentially Sizable Health Benefit' of Alcohol" and "Study Finds Better Brain Functioning Among Moderate Alcohol Consuming Women."

Internet resources

Alcohol: Problems and Solutions Website
website: www2.potsdam.edu/alcohol-info

This website describes alcohol use and abuse along with effective ways to reduce or eliminate drinking problems such as underage drinking, drinking and driving, and binge drinking. The "In Their Own Words" section contains interviews with experts on a wide variety of alcohol-related issues, "In the News" provides current news articles for downloading, and "In My Opinion" offers essays including "It's Better to Teach Safe Use of Alcohol."

College Alcohol Study (CAS)
Website: www.hsph.harvard.edu

The College Alcohol Study (CAS), a project of the Harvard School of Public Health, is a large and ongoing survey of the drinking habits of college students. Its website provides articles and reports based on this research, as well as a place to submit queries about college students and alcohol abuse.

Drink Smart
website: www.drinksmart.org

Drink Smart is an electronic magazine, based in Canada, that believes encouraging responsible drinking by young people who have reached the legal age is a laudable goal. Drink Smart publishes personal stories on drinking and driving, the effects of alcohol and families, and attitudes towards drinking among teens and at colleges.

The Stanton Peele Addiction Website
website: www.peele.net

Stanton Peele has been researching and writing about addiction for thirty years. His controversial approach negates the American medical model of addiction as a disease. Instead, he views it as a behavior which can be overcome through maturity, improved coping skills, and better self-management and self-esteem. His website includes an "Ask Stanton" question and answer section and an extensive virtual library of articles available for viewing. Peele has also authored several books, including *The Truth About Addiction and Recovery* and *Diseasing of America*, which may be ordered from the website.

Bibliography

Books

Sylvia Cary	*Women Celebrate Long-Term Sobriety: Sober Women Share About Life, Love, Family, Work and Money.* Los Angeles: Lowell House, 1999.
Karen Casey	*The Miracle of Sponsorship: Recovery Stories of Hope and Renewal.* Center City, MN: Hazelden, 2000.
Christina Chiu	*Teen Guide to Staying Sober.* New York: Rosen, 1998.
Irving A. Cohen	*Addiction: The High-Low Trap.* Santa Fe, NM: Health Press, 1995.
Barbara S. Cole	*Gifts of Sobriety: When the Promises of Recovery Come True.* Center City, MN: Hazelden, 2000.
D.J. Cornett	*Seven Weeks to Safe Social Drinking: How to Effectively Moderate Your Alcohol Intake.* Secaucus, NJ: Carol Publishing Group, 1997.
Anne M. Fletcher	*Sober for Good: New Solutions for Drinking Problems— Advice from Those Who Have Succeeded.* New York: Houghton Mifflin Company, 2001.
Marianne Gilliam	*How Alcoholics Anonymous Failed Me: My Personal Journey to Sobriety Through Self-Empowerment.* New York: William and Morrow Company, 1998.
David J. Hanson	*Alcohol Education: What We Must Do.* Westport, CT: Praeger, 1996.
Michael Hardiman	*Overcoming Addiction: A Common Sense Approach.* Freedom, CA: Crossing Press, 2000.
Jonathan Harris	*This Drinking Nation.* New York: Simon and Schuster, 1994.
Devon Jersild	*Happy Hours: Alcohol in a Woman's Life.* New York: Cliff Street Books, 2001.
Katherine Ketcham and William F. Asbury	*Beyond the Influence: Understanding and Defeating Alcoholism.* New York: Bantam Books, 2000.
Audrey Kishline	*Moderate Drinking: The Moderation Management Guide for People Who Want to Reduce Their Drinking.* New York: Crown, 1996.
Joan Mathews Larson	*Seven Weeks to Sobriety: The Proven Program to Fight Alcoholism Through Nutrition.* New York: Ballantine Wellspring, 1997.
Alagna Magdalena and Ruth Anne Ruiz	*Everything You Need to Know About the Dangers of Binge Drinking.* New York: Rosen, 2001.

John Michael — *The Art of Moderation: An Alternative to Alcoholism.* Mill Valley, CA: Vision Books International, 1999.

Craig Nakken — *Reclaim Your Family from Addiction: How Couples and Families Recover Love and Meaning.* Center City, MN: Hazelden, 2000.

Hank Nuwer — *Wrongs of Passage: Fraternities, Sororities, Hazing, and Binge Drinking.* Bloomington: Indiana University Press, 1999.

Edmund B. O'Reilly — *Sobering Tales: Narratives of Alcoholism and Recovery.* Amherst: University of Massachusetts Press, 1997.

Stanton Peele — *Diseasing of America: How We Allowed Recovery Zealots and the Treatment Industry to Convince Us We Are Out of Control.* San Francisco: Jossey-Bass, 1999.

David Earl Thomson — *A Fellowship of Men and Women.* New York: ExCel, 1999.

Jack Trimpey — *Rational Recovery: The New Cure for Substance Addiction.* New York: Pocket Books, 1996.

William L. White — *Slaying the Dragon: The History of Addiction Treatment and Recovery in America.* Bloomington, IL: Chestnut Health Systems/Lighthouse Institute, 1998.

Periodicals

Susan Brink — "How to Help an Alcoholic," *U.S. News & World Report,* May 7, 2001.

Susan Brink — "Your Brain on Alcohol," *U.S. News & World Report,* May 7, 2001.

Jane E. Brody — "Masters Show How to Get High on Life Without Abusing Alcohol," *New York Times,* April 24, 2001.

William F. Buckley Jr. — "On the Right—Let's Drink to It," *National Review,* April 2, 2001.

David Byrd — "Last Call for Alcohol?" *National Journal,* December 18, 1999.

CQ Researcher — "Drinking on Campus," March 20, 1998. Available from 22nd St. NW, Washington, DC 20037.

Sean Elder — "Last Call," *Men's Health,* April 2001.

Michael P. Haines — "Facts Change Student Drinking," *USA Today,* July 23, 2001.

Walter Kim — "What Do You Tell the Kids? How a Recovering Alcoholic Plans to Urge His Daughter to Abstain," *Time,* June 18, 2001.

Karl E. Miller — "Naltrexone Effective in Treatment of Alcoholism," *American Family Physician,* February 15, 2000.

Eric Nagourney — "A Generational Link to Alcohol Abuse," *New York Times,* June 26, 2001.

Hans S. Nichols — "Getting Drunk on Rebellion," *Insight on the News,* July 16, 2001.

Don Oldenburg   "Kids and Alcohol: A Controversial Alternative to 'Just Say No,'" *Washington Post*, March 10, 1998.

John O'Neil   "For Drinkers, Intervention in the E.R." *New York Times*, January 22, 2001.

Naomi Schaefer   "Campus Crackdown," *National Review*, April 5, 1999.

Debbie Seaman   "I Finally Quit Drinking," *Ladies' Home Journal*, May 2001.

Nancy Wartik   "Paying a Price for Drinking Men Under the Table," *New York Times*, June 24, 2001.

Henry Wechsler   "Binge Drinking: Should We Attack the Name or the Problem?" *Chronicle of Higher Education*, October 20, 2000.

Bernice Wuethrich   "Getting Stupid: Effects of Alcohol Abuse on Teenagers," *Discover*, March 2001.

Kate Zernike   "New Tactic on College Drinking: Play It Down," *New York Times*, October 3, 2000.

Index

AA. *See* Alcoholics Anonymous
adopted children, 11
alcohol abuse
  vs. alcoholism, 6
  defined, 6
  health problems associated
    with, 53
  statistics, 6
  see also alcoholism; binge
    drinking
Alcoholics Anonymous (AA)
  on controlled drinking, 60
  as a fellowship, 21
  finances, 23
  indoctrination through, 26
  lack of religious affiliation in,
    24
  membership obligations, 20–21,
    22–23
  as misleading, 29
  vs. moderation drinking, 31
  philosophy of, 7
  recovery rate under, 7–8
  religion of, 28
  vs. self-reliance, 27
  sharing experiences through,
    21–22
  sobriety as sole purpose of,
    24–25
  working together in, 22
alcoholism
  vs. alcohol abuse, 6
  alternative model to, 19
  as a disease, 6–7, 14–15
    compassionate treatment and,
      16–17
    historical perspective on,
      15–16

public opinion on, 10
research supporting, 10–13
as a personal weakness, 10–12
political consequences of,
  18–19
vs. problem drinking, 36–37
psychological consequences of,
  17–18
social consequences of, 17
see also alcohol abuse
alcohol overdoses, 41, 45–46
alcohol use
  for celebration, 6
  harmful consequences of, 50–51
  Prohibition and, 51–53
  see also binge drinking
Alexander, F., 8
Antabuse (medication), 56–58,
  60–62
antidepressant medication, 56
Asbury, William F., 9

Begleiter, Henri, 11
binge drinking
  alcohol education for, 42
  college responses to, 40–41, 51
  efforts to control and punish,
    49–50
  low-cost alcohol as factor in,
    44–45
  vs. moderation drinking, 53–54
  nonbinge drinkers and, 43–44
  of-age students enabling, 46
  peer support for, 45–46
  problems associated with, 41
  social pressures and, 48–49
  strict campus policies for, 42–43
  student rights and, 46–47

variations within colleges and,
41–42
Blum, Kenneth, 10–11, 12

Chace, Thomas Curtis, 20
Ciaramicoli, Arthur P., 9
Civelli, Olivier, 12
College Alcohol Study (CAS), 40
college students. *See* binge
drinking

deaths, alcohol overdoses, 41,
45–46
DeLuca, Alexander, 38
Dreyfus, Edward A., 14
drug therapy
Antabuse, 56–58
dealing with sobriety combined
with, 58–60
history of, 55–56
objections to, 60–62
time allotted for, 60
drunk driving, 6
moderation drinking and,
31–32, 33–34, 37
peer support for, 45

education, alcohol, 42

Fingarette, Herbert, 7

Geller, Irving, 10
Goodwin, Donald W., 11, 55
Gordis, Enoch, 37
Gould, Meredith, 7

Harden, Mike, 30

Jellinek, Elvin M., 6

Ketcham, Katherine, 9
Kishline, Audrey, 30–32, 33–34,
35, 37
Knapp, Caroline, 36

Krohn, Franklin B., 48

moderation drinking
vs. abstinence, 36–37
auto accidents and, 31–32, 33
vs. binge drinking by college
students, 53–54
defined, 53
evidence supporting, 37–38
for problem drinkers, 35–36
vs. recovery programs, 30–31
spokesperson for, 30, 33–34

National Council on Alcohol and
Drug Dependence (NCADD),
34, 37
National Institute on Alcohol
Abuse and Alcoholism (NIAAA),
6, 37–38
NCADD. *See* National Council on
Alcohol and Drug Dependence
Nelson, Toben, 40
Noble, Ernest, 12

overdose deaths, 41, 45–46

Peele, Stanton, 8, 33
Pendery, Mary, 35
Prohibition, 51–53
Project MATCH, 37

research
on abstinence vs. moderation
techniques, 35
on controlled drinking, 37–38
supporting hereditary factors of
alcoholism, 10–13
Rollins, M., 8

Schulstad, Mel, 9
sexual assault, 46
Smithers, R. Brinkley, 38–39
Smithers-Fornaci, Adele, 38
Sobell, Linda, 35

Sobell, Mark, 35

treatment
  abstinence vs. moderation
    drinking, 7–8, 30–32, 34–35,
    38
  based on disease theory, 6–7
  for problems drinkers vs.
    alcoholics, 35–37
  see also drug therapy
Trimpey, Jack, 26

U.S. Drug-Free Schools and
  Communities Act Amendment
  (1989), 51

Wechsler, Henry, 40
Weitzman, Elissa R., 40

Yale Center of Alcoholic Studies,
  10